The ***Specific*** ***EDGE***

How Sustained Effort Wins in Business and Life

Mike Wien

ISBN: 978-0-9907686-0-9

Library of Congress Control Number: 2014915579

Cover design: Peri-Poloni Gabriel, Knockout Design
Cover photo: © FinisherPix.com
Interior formatting: Vanessa Lowry, Connect 4 Leverage

First Edition Printed, 2014

This book may be purchased in bulk for educational, business, fundraising, or sales promotional use. For information please contact: Mike Wien, www.MikeWien.com, mike@specificedge.com

Printed in the United States of America

▲

This book is dedicated to my closest family members.

To Mim and Bob Wien, my mother and father, who taught me how to be a competitor; not just how to win, but how to appreciate the accomplishments of others, learn from defeat, and do the right thing.

To Nannette Wien, my wife of thirty-nine years, who is my biggest cheerleader and is always there to help me on my journey.

To Andrew and Jason Wien, our second and third sons, who are my primary reason for keeping in shape and staying young—so I can still keep up with them!

To Anita and Byron Wien, my aunt and uncle, who taught me and my family the importance of concentration and discipline.

And to our oldest son Brian, who helped me understand the significance of living a balanced life and who taught me the importance of celebrating every accomplishment and milestone along the way.

▲▲▲

*Success is best built by those
who turn obstacles,
failures, and disappointments
into learning experiences
for moving forward.*

MIKE WIEN

▲

Table of Contents

It is not how good you are,
it is how good you try to be.

MIKE WIEN

▲

Acknowledgments

As with most accomplishments, this book would not have happened without the support and encouragement of many people in my life. I would like to thank the following individuals who played a role in helping me develop this book by challenging me to hone my own Specific Edge and reminding me that Sustained Effort Wins!

Thank you to Sam Horn, who helped me develop the Specific Edge concept, and to Mark Levy, who helped me better understand the true driver of success: overcoming obstacles, setbacks, and failures.

Thank you to all of my training buddies who encouraged me to train harder and more often, and who helped me celebrate my successes and learn from setbacks. They include the TriGeeks led by Fox Ferrel along with Jim and Mary Duguay, the Monday-night running group led by Adri Herman, the Thursday-morning track workout led by Debbie Alexander, the Atlanta Track Club Masters Team led by Malcolm Campbell and Kirk Larson, and the Concourse masters swim team coached by Pete Farren, Oliver Gumbrill, and Megan Melgaard.

I'm grateful to my triathlete training buddies who are also businessmen during the day, including Jack Spartz, Dick Jones, Scott Boylan, Bishop Leatherbury, Ralph Bower, Lewis Shubin, Calvin Gray, Mike Allpass, Gary Kessler, Chuck Bengochea, Bill McDonough, Jon Chamberlain, David Daggett, Richard Yow, Larry Anspach, and Leslie Zacks. You proved to be great sounding boards as I worked to make connections between triathlons and business development.

Thank you to my nephew David Salzman and my niece Ashley Simon Brooks, who are members of both my family and the Ironman-finishers family.

To my fellow professional speakers including Paul Schempp, Rob "Waldo" Waldman, Dan Thurman, Martha Lanier, Jonathan Schwartz, Ken Futch, and Jack Daly, thank you for encouraging me to share my story and make a difference.

I am grateful to my business mentors, including Alan Cohen, Allen Soden, Mike Leven, and Ron Tidmore.

To Debby Cannon, Director of the Hospitality School at Georgia State University for her encouragement and Tom Breedlove, Jill Kersh, Joe Hardy, Kayla Napier, and Danica Forshner for their creative suggestions.

To Mike Lenhart, Richard Anton, and Barry Siff, I am thankful for your support in getting me involved with the USA Triathlon board of directors.

Thank you to my coaches, Gerry Halpen, Dan Wisnewski, and Melvin Edwards.

My Timex Multisport Team mates led by Tristan Brown and Sam Martin also have my gratitude.

Finally, thank you to Helen Chang, Kristine Serio, and the Author Bridge Media team for your editorial and publishing services. Your most valuable contribution was in the insightful questions you asked that stimulated additional ideas and helped add clarity and depth to the points I was making.

The Power Of Focused Effort

You just can't beat the person who never gives up.

BABE RUTH

What Is Success?

What is success? And who is successful?

Whether you're talking about sports, business, or anything else in life, the same key elements underlie success. Success isn't marked by the fastest, the smartest, or the brightest person in the room. It's not always the result of natural talent. Most of the time, those things have nothing to do with it.

Successful people are just good at moving forward. They're people with goals. They're people who understand how to overcome setbacks. They don't have a magic formula.

They have willpower.

This book is for entrepreneurs: people responsible for growing a business. Maybe you're a new business owner. Maybe you're a corporate executive. Maybe you're a partner in a firm. You need to be creative, help your organization thrive, and set the tone for a department. You need to help people overcome obstacles to find success.

I found my way to success that same way. As a kid, I wasn't a natural-born superstar. I was a late bloomer. I probably spent more time in detention than I did inside the classroom during my first seven years at school. In sports, I played right field—the designated position for the worst kid on the team. When a ball flew to right field, two people were always petrified: the coach and me. We both knew I could get hurt.

Fast-forward fifty years. I now lead an exciting and purposeful life. I am a top Ironman triathlete, an executive who has led some of the largest brands in the world, a sought-after speaker, and a marketing professor at Georgia State University.

How did I get here? Not with my inborn star power. I got here because I worked hard. I got here because I set goals. I got here because I had the discipline and the focus to follow through with my dreams.

Most of all, I got here because I figured out how to convert setbacks into learning experiences. I was better at that than anything else. When things went wrong, I recognized new opportunities. I was open-minded enough to change with the market.

That was the key on my path to success.

Step It Up

Most entrepreneurs know how to start. You spot a great opportunity, and you seize it. You make some money. You see some success.

And then you hit a wall.

You realize that to keep growing, you've got to step it up. But you don't know how. You started with a great idea, but you never had a master plan. Suddenly, you're overwhelmed. Obstacles are flying at you left and right. You're working yourself to death, and you're out of balance. You can't delegate tasks to anybody else because if you don't do them yourself, you're sure the business will fail.

Part of you still thinks you know what you're doing. You started this thing. Why take advice from other people on how to run it? Meanwhile, your balance sheet is your checking account. Your cash flow is how much money you have in the bank. You don't plan, because you figure that you can't predict the future anyway. Your marketing strategy is "word of mouth." You don't hold yourself accountable, because you don't know what to hold yourself accountable for.

Or maybe you're just stuck in the same routine. Your business is chugging along. You're doing all right financially, but you sense that you haven't reached your full potential.

You know you can do better. You just don't know how to move forward.

This is the make-or-break stage of business. You need to change or face the consequences. The old model is going to burn you out. Your business and your personal life will fall apart.

Maybe you're used to picking yourself back up when you're down. But unless you follow the right principles, you're going to hit the point where you just can't get back up again.

You're ready to transition from the "gut reaction" method to the "sustainable process" way of running your business. You're ready to turn "some" success into lifelong success. You're ready to get the confidence, the patience, and the tools you need to take this business to the next level. You're ready to put yourself in control of your vision and live a more purposeful life.

You're ready to develop your specific edge.

The Specific Edge

The Specific Edge is about constancy and creativity. It's about making mid-course corrections to find the best opportunities. When you have a specific edge, you're in tune with yourself, the changing market, and the opportunities around you. You have a vision, a dream, a set of long-term goals that you're passionate about. That vision is so powerful that it helps you overcome anything in your way.

When you take your specific edge to heart, you put the power of focused effort in your hands. You make the changes you need to make to reach your long-term goal. You understand that there will be bumps in the road, and that you may fall off your ideal timetable.

But you keep moving toward your destination anyway.

You're committed 100 percent to your long-term journey. Your focus is unshakable. Discipline, concentration, and endurance all factor in to your decisions. You understand that there's no such thing as an overnight success. In business, in athletics, and in life, real success takes real commitment.

Real success takes a specific edge.

Specialize to Succeed: Ironman

When you put enough sustained, specialized focus on something, anything is possible.

That's true of business, and it's true of life as well. One of my favorite examples of this is the Ironman World Championship.

The Ironman triathlon is a grueling course of swimming, biking, and running raced over seventeen hours maximum. The swim is

2.4 miles, the bike is 112 miles, and the run is 26.2 miles long. One of my most satisfying personal achievements is that I took second place in the Ironman World Championship for my age group in 2011. When I look back on that accomplishment, the parallels between success in that triathlon and success in the business world are almost endless.

Success in an Ironman is not about inborn talent. It's about putting in the time to specialize. It's about defining what you are good at and passionate about doing. It's about building skills and endurance. It's about overcoming the hurdles that cross your path—anything from injuries to bad weather. It's about having discipline, showing up, and staying in the race to the end.

The Specific Edge is the culmination of my twenty-eight years of working at major corporations and my decade of training for the Ironman triathlon. Going through those things made it clear to me that my success wasn't beyond my control. Success lay in my ability to overcome obstacles, learn from mistakes, and keep moving. It lay in my ability to hone my focus and leverage it to my advantage. It lay in my ability to harness the power of my specific edge.

Success is defined by each of us. It is the foundation of a meaningful and purposeful life. At the business level, it means growing your business to boundless new heights. But however you define it, the key to success is already in your hands.

The key to success is your specific edge.

Be the Best at Something, Not Everything

Very few people can be really good at everything. The people who really excel are the ones who become experts at something very specific. These are the people who target success.

For me, success was never a question of being the best in every field. It was the realization that being the best didn't mean I had to be the best at everything. More than that, the things I excelled at were the things I already enjoyed doing. When I put my focus on them, it brought great satisfaction to my life and ultimately made me successful.

You need to create your own competitive advantage—your specific edge. Whether your goal is winning a race or achieving success in the business world, you have to set yourself apart. You do that by figuring out what your specific edge is, and you find it by playing to your strengths. You have to be passionate. You have to focus on what you enjoy. You have to discipline yourself to become the best in your class.

When you put your focus on what you're good at and hone that skill, you find more than just success. You find happiness, fulfillment, and purpose.

My Story

My story didn't start with amazing luck and silver spoons. As I said, I was a late bloomer. That was true in business as well as athletics. I was average. And average doesn't stand out.

Then after I'd been working for a few years, I finally discovered some things that I both enjoyed and was good at. I found them in sports, and I found them in business.

In sports, I enjoyed running, but my legs couldn't handle as much of it as they grew older. So I started some cross-training to stay fit. I biked. I swam. And I realized that I wasn't half bad at that combination: running, biking, and swimming. My greatest strength was endurance. The longer the distance, the better I did. Before I knew it, I had migrated to the Ironman triathlon, a journey that eventually led me to my second-place finish in the world championship.

My career evolved like the triathlon did. After I earned my MBA, I went to work for Frito-Lay and PepsiCo. I was pretty good at analyzing numbers, and Frito-Lay had purchased a mainframe computer to run some detailed sales statistics. This was before the personal computer had been invented, so just having access to that computer terminal was a big step forward in my career.

Before long I had an opportunity to launch a new product at the company: a salty snack called Fantastix. Fantastix turned out to be the biggest disaster that Frito-Lay has ever seen. I learned from that experience. The next product I launched was the most successful food brand of the 1970s and is still on the market thirty-five years later.

That product is Tostitos.

No part of my formula for success is theory. I've lived it. Success is built on your ability to handle challenges, get up when you're down, and convert your bad days into learning experiences. Success is built with each step you take to keep moving forward.

Success is built into your specific edge.

Specific Edge Coach

Over ten years ago, I left the corporate world to put the strategies you're about to learn into play in my personal life. I didn't have names for them at the time. I just knew that I wanted to go after the things I was most passionate about. And I did.

In 2003, I became a consultant to entrepreneurial organizations and individuals. I showed my clients how to apply the same successful marketing principles used by the big boys to their own businesses. I've spent twenty-eight years flourishing in corporate America, and another ten transforming myself from an average athlete into one of the best triathletes in the world. Thanks to those experiences, I've been able to help hundreds of people and companies create specific edges for themselves, even when they didn't have a big budget to work with.

As a professor of marketing in the Cecil B. Day School of Hospitality Administration at Georgia State University, I teach my students the strategies they need to find success every year. Those students enter the market with the tools to create competitive advantages for their businesses. They enter the market prepared to make a difference in the world.

My students, my business clients, and my athlete mentees are living the promise of *The Specific Edge*.

Road Map to Success

This book is a road map. It is a blueprint for how the average person can achieve success, fulfillment, and purpose that is far above average.

Most people are not born "winners." Most people did not get the best grades, go to the best schools, or have all the luck. But most successful people didn't get where they are because of those things. Most successful people got where they are because they had the willpower to do three things.

Show up. Woody Allen said it best: "Eighty percent of being successful is showing up." You have control over your future. Pick something you love to do, then show up every day and do it.

Focus on what you're good at. Take your passion, that thing you're naturally good at, and turn it into your specialization. Focus on making yourself the best of the best in your area of expertise.

Be strategic. Finally, leverage your specialization to take yourself where you want to go. Set goals. Practice discipline. Maintain balance and a positive attitude, and anticipate where the next step to success will take you.

A lot of successful people got where they are because they specialized and worked hard. They had a dream, and they were passionate about it. They didn't let setbacks throw them off course. Instead, they converted their challenges into learning experiences and kept moving forward.

You have more control over your destiny than many people give you credit for. That's the ultimate lesson of *The Specific Edge*.

How to Read This Book

The Specific Edge is the type of book you read from start to finish. But it's a book about evolution, not revolution.

Principles like these aren't something you can absorb in one day. You don't read through them, take notes, and then wake up the next morning saying, "Okay, I read the book. Today, everything changes." Instead, start by focusing on one concept. Tell yourself, "I'm going to set some very specific goals and share them with everyone." Then let that step lead you to the next opportunity.

The Specific Edge is a step-by-step blueprint for success. Learn the concepts in sequence first. Then take your time living them out one by one. When you need a refresher, go back and refer to the chapter you're working on. Come back to this book when you experience a major setback. Use its principles to help you persevere toward your ultimate goal.

If you're an individual looking to build your career, this book will teach you how to take advantage of the power you already possess.

If you're a leader in an organization, the same principles can be leveraged to help your company grow to new heights.

This is not just a book you read. This is a book you bring to life one value at a time.

A Specific Edge Wins You Success

When you apply the principles in this book, your life will undergo a revolution. You will live each day with greater purpose. You will differentiate yourself from the rest of the market with a competitive advantage. You will find the motivation to show up every day, hang on to your vision, and keep yourself moving forward. You will be happier, because you'll be doing something you're passionate about. You will make a difference in other people's lives.

You will get where you want to go, and you will achieve success.

The advantage of a specific edge lies in the focus and endurance it gives you to work toward your long-term goals. Whether you are running a business or a triathlon, you can excel. You can put yourself on the podium, no matter where you came from or what you want to do.

You can live the reality of your specific edge. And the first step on that journey is visualizing your goals and dreams.

▲

CHAPTER ONE

The Edge Of Goals And Dreams

A dream doesn't become reality through magic; it takes sweat, determination, and hard work.

COLIN POWELL

The Tear Test

I once spoke to a group of students in a running program. These kids came from very difficult and challenging backgrounds. They were in the running program because a judge had recommended it. Running was a tool to help them develop discipline, concentration, and endurance.

I was the guest speaker at their awards banquet. The kids themselves were seated in the front of the room, and their parents filled the back tables. I gave them my speech about the power of a specific edge and how sustained effort wins, and one of the things I talked about was setting goals and dreams.

"You have to put your dreams through the tear test," I said. All twenty-five of their faces were on me, listening. "When you think about accomplishing your dream, it should bring a tear to your eye. Maybe one of your dreams is to be the first member of your family to graduate from college. If you can visualize walking down the aisle in your cap and gown at your college graduation, and if that brings a tear to your eye, then it qualifies. It passes the tear test."

At that moment, I looked over the students to where their parents were sitting in the back of the room. All of them were drying their eyes with their napkins. For them, that was a long-term goal that resonated.

That dream passed the tear test.

The Lighthouse: Goals and Dreams

The road to success is about persistence, endurance, and moving forward. The entrepreneurs and organizations on that road can walk it because they understand where they're going long term.

They can walk it because they have goals and dreams.

The journey of honing a specific edge implies that you want to reach a particular destination. That destination is your success. When you set a goal or a dream, you are defining exactly what that success is. You're being specific and purposeful about what you want to accomplish.

You're taking the first step on your journey to success.

Setting a goal and a dream is a critical element of success. Goals and dreams steer us toward a larger purpose. They keep us focused on what we really want. They push us to think about the long term instead of the short term. They break big concepts down into milestones that we can work toward and celebrate along the way. And sometimes they lead us to mid-course corrections that help us define better goals and dreams that we never saw coming.

Goals and dreams are your lighthouse. They are your north star. When you have strong goals, you can navigate through the short-term setbacks that you encounter on the way to your destination.

You have to be passionate about your goals. The right dream will always pass the tear test. When I set my goal to finish in the top five of the Ironman World Championship, the vision of crossing that finish line brought a tear to my eye. Turning that dream into a reality became my driving force.

Your goals always answer the question, "What's in it for me?" That's true from both a personal and corporate standpoint. If you're leading a business, your goals are even bigger. They're also about what's in it for the customer, what's in it for the employees, and what's in it for the shareholders. How does your goal help those people? How does it improve their lives? If you can put those considerations in place, you have more than a good goal. You have a very successful and profitable organization.

As an entrepreneur, your goals need to be visionary and aspirational. They need to be bigger than just driving the stock price this quarter. You have to want to make a difference in your customers' lives. You have to want to find solutions to their problems. Those are the kinds of goals that keep you focused and keep your people motivated to come to work every day.

One great example of this is Tom's Shoes. The people at Tom's Shoes build really stylish and comfortable shoes, but they don't stop there. Their goal is to make a difference in the world. For every pair of shoes they sell, they donate a pair to someone in a developing country. They call it "One for One."

By 2013, Tom's Shoes had given away ten million pairs of shoes. The company was certainly helping its bottom line and growing as a business, but it was also making a difference—and not just to the people in need of shoes. The program also makes the customers feel good about buying Tom's Shoes. It makes the employees passionate about the company they work for.

That's a powerful dream.

Goals and dreams need to be specific and realistic. They need to have passion. They need to have milestones and accountability. They need to be shared with others, and they need to embody an inspirational long-term vision. You have to stay connected to your dreams, and you have to celebrate the progress you make on the path to achieving them. You have to take ownership of your goals so that they truly belong to you, not to your parents, your spouse, your co-workers, or your CEO.

Your dreams need to drive you to the finish line of your success.

Quantify Your Goals

I use the terms "goals" and "dreams" interchangeably, but I make a slight distinction between them. Goals are the technical side of an objective, and dreams are the emotional side of it. Ambiguity has no place with either of them. For a goal to be truly real, it has to be quantified.

Say you want to lose weight. It's not enough just to state, "I want to lose weight." You need to make that goal quantifiable by attaching a specific number to it. What you should say instead is, "I want to lose fifty pounds."

As an entrepreneur, your goals need to follow the same rule. You never say, "I want to increase revenues." You say, "I want to bring in $1 million in new client relationships by the end of the year." Not, "I want to grow my business," but "I want to grow my business from the fifth-largest company in the industry to the third-largest in the industry."

Once you have your specific, quantifiable goal, the next step is to "eat the elephant one bite at a time." Break your goal up into bite-sized pieces—or milestones. Your milestones also need to be specific and quantifiable. When you write them out, they should look like this: "To bring in $1 million in new client relationships by the end of the year, I need to identify four new prospects per month, schedule relationship-development meetings with two of them, identify a significant service they need that costs $100,000 or more, and start providing that service to at least one of the two potentials I met with."

Specific, quantifiable goals come with one huge advantage: they can be tracked. When you track your goals, you can figure out exactly what steps you need to take along the road to your final destination. You can create a system to make yourself and others accountable for progress. You can celebrate successes along the way. And you can keep the whole team engaged as you work toward your collective benchmarks.

How do you transform non-specific intentions into effective business goals? Follow these examples.

Human Resources

WEAK: I want to develop a culture that attracts the best people for the job.

STRONG: I want to develop and implement a program this year that creates a new culture in my company—one that attracts and retains the best and the brightest talent. To measure the success of this goal, I want us to be listed in the local business magazine's top ten companies to work for at the end of year.

Promotion

WEAK: I want to be promoted to partner in the shortest amount of time possible.

STRONG: I want to be promoted to partner in the next two years, and I'll make that happen by developing my own clients and bringing in at least 50 percent of what I work on. I won't rely on others in the firm to give me work.

Job Seeker

WEAK: I want to find a job to support my family.

STRONG: I want to find a new job in the next three months, and I want it to be a position where I can leverage my sales experience providing technology solutions to organizations in the healthcare industry.

Sales

WEAK: I want to come out of the recession and return to a growth company.

STRONG: I want to grow my business by 20 percent next year. I want 5 percent of that growth to come from opening a new office, 5 percent to come from attracting new clients to our existing offices, and 10 percent to come from deepening relationships with existing customers.

Share Your Dreams

When you share your goals with others, you motivate yourself to accomplish what you set out to do. The more people you share your dreams with, the more support you'll have on your journey. You won't want to let them down, and you can leverage that pressure to achieve success.

My father was in the United States Navy during World War II. He spent a couple of years chasing Japanese submarines in the middle of the Pacific. When he came back from that experience in 1945 at the age of twenty, he was addicted to smoking. One day, nine years later, he decided to quit cold turkey. Back in 1954, few people were worried about the effect that smoking had on your health, and even fewer chose to quit. But my dad had a goal to quit smoking, and he shared that goal with everyone he knew.

The pressure not to fail them proved greater than his desire to have a cigarette. He never smoked again.

Sharing your dreams is just as effective in the business world. When I worked at Frito-Lay, my mentor was Roger Enrico. Roger was the director of marketing for all corn-based brands at the time, but he had a dream of one day running PepsiCo—Frito-Lay's parent company. He wanted to create an organization that attracted the best and the brightest. He wanted people who would help Frito-Lay's customers—the store owners—to develop thriving businesses.

Roger didn't keep his dream to himself. He made sure we all knew what he wanted to achieve. And because he did that, everyone around him supported his goal. The people above him recognized his talent and passion. His peers and the people in his department knew that they were working with someone special, and they gave it their all.

I followed Roger Enrico's career for many years. When he retired, he was the chairman of PepsiCo. That's the power of sharing your dreams.

Make Your People Part of Your Dream

As an entrepreneur and a leader, it's your responsibility to translate your dreams and goals down to everyone in your organization. Every person on your team needs to understand your long-term vision, as well as his or her specific role in helping the organization reach that benchmark.

Your team members need to buy into your dream. They need to have a vested interest in what you're fighting for. They need to have a burning desire to be a part of the organization's long-term success.

Why? Because when your team is invested in your dream, that dream takes on a life of its own. It is no longer your goal, but the team's goal. They own it. They will track results and motivate themselves to keep moving forward. They will find solutions to problems that get in the way. They will be the first to celebrate successes, and they will have the satisfaction of making a difference to a winning team. Best of all, they will do all of this with very little input or management from you.

The dream becomes their idea and their victory. And in the end, you are the biggest beneficiary.

For instance, say your goal is to grow sales. You know that one of the key ways you can differentiate yourself from your competition is through customer service: by understanding the needs of your customers better than anyone else. That means that everyone in the company needs to give superior customer service by anticipating the customer's needs.

If you can get each member of your company to buy into the reason for superior customer service—your bigger joint goal—then those people will become part of your dream. When they become part of your dream, they'll care about making that dream a reality.

Most people in an organization don't know or understand what they can do to help grow the company's stock price. What matters to them is making a difference that they can see for themselves. They want to play a part in turning a dream into a reality. They want to know what they can do within their spheres of influence to make a difference.

Reinvent Your Goals and Dreams

A goal or a dream might be a fixed concept. But setting dreams and goals should be an ongoing life practice.

You have to be open minded. You have to be willing to adjust your goals and dreams if you need to. Maybe you'll run into a change in the market. Maybe a new opportunity will come up that wasn't there before. Maybe the trends will change for your industry. Maybe you'll realize that your skills will get better recognition somewhere else. Reinventing your dreams and goals is sometimes the best way to keep them alive.

In 2001, four things happened that forced me to rethink my priorities. I was a partner at Deloitte, heading up our industry marketing efforts, when they fell like a line of dominos. First, Arthur Anderson, one of our biggest competitors, closed its doors. Second, our largest office in New York with 3,500 employees had to be relocated because it was right across the street from the World Trade Center at the time of the September 11 terrorist attacks. Third, Congress passed a bill that made a big part of my job—selling additional services to our clients—illegal. And fourth, my mentor and boss at Deloitte had a heart attack and stepped down from head of marketing.

I sensed it was time to reinvent myself. One year later, I left Deloitte to pursue three dreams. I joined Georgia State University as an adjunct professor. I started my own firm that focused on professional speaking and consulting. And I began an aggressive training program to compete in the Ironman triathlon.

I focused on the things I was naturally good at and enjoyed. I did activities that I was passionate about. I developed a flexible career that gave me more time to spend with my family and friends.

I adopted a lifestyle that was more consistent with my long-term dream.

Not every adjustment you have to make to your dreams will be pleasant. After I took second at the Ironman World Championship,

I failed to qualify for the championships at all two years later. That was a wake-up call for me. I wandered around for a full week after that disappointment with no defined direction.

Then my nephew called and said that he was going to do the Ironman in Mont-Tremblant the following August—did I want to join him? I thought about it and agreed to participate. As soon as I signed up, my new goal changed my whole mindset. I went back to my exercise routine with passion and energy.

Once you fulfill a goal, come up with a new one. When you learn how to do that, you'll never lose your purpose.

Dreams that Leverage Your Specific Edge

In 2014, I spent fifteen days in Colorado with my two sons, Andrew and Jason. Andrew was twenty-seven, and Jason was twenty-three. I was sixty-two. For two weeks, I chased them down expert runs. All three of us appreciated how special it was that I could keep up with them at a peer level. That's always been my real driver for staying in great shape: to be able to experience life to the fullest with my sons.

The difference between people who have goals and people who don't is that the people with goals live their lives with purpose. People without goals and dreams live by default. Their focus in life is just to make it through the day. In most cases, they achieve that modest goal, but they have little reason to be enthusiastic about their lives.

Then you have people who embrace strong goals and dreams. These are the people who wake up each day with excitement. They're the ones who are always ready to develop a new idea, to create a new product, to learn a new skill, or to explore a new area of their field.

They're the people who make a real difference in this world. And by setting your own visionary goals and dreams, you have the power to be one of them.

Once your goal is clearly defined, you're ready to start working toward it. The first step of that process is specialization.

▲

CHAPTER TWO
Cutting-Edge Specialization

Each man is capable of doing one thing well. If he attempts several, he will fail to achieve distinction in any.

PLATO

Cab Drivers for Businesspeople

Over the years, I've been through some tiring business trips. Anybody who has traveled for business can relate to this. You've been at meetings all day, and after they're finally over you rush to catch a late flight to another city. By the time you land, you're completely drained; and you still have to make it through the cab ride to your hotel.

One of these trips in particular I will never forget. I was flying into New York. It was 10:30 p.m., and I was exhausted. I fell into a cab and told the driver the name of my hotel in Manhattan.

Instead of just ignoring me and getting on the road, he turned around and looked at me sitting in the backseat. "Boy," he said, "it looks like you've had a busy day. Do you mind if I play some music? You just sit back there and relax."

"Okay, sure," I said.

He put on a beautiful, soothing operatic CD. He had a couple of nice speakers in the back. And suddenly I was in an environment that was so peaceful and calm that frankly I didn't care where he drove me. I was so comfortable and relaxed.

By the time we got to the hotel, I didn't even want to get out of the cab. I was enjoying the CD too much. "Who is this artist?" I asked him.

"Her name's Sarah Brightman," he told me.

I made a note of that so that I'd be able to buy the music myself later. And when I got out of the cab, I gave the driver a tip that was almost as much as the fare itself.

The cab driver I met that day had obviously driven his share of tired businesspeople. In fact, he probably made a point of focusing on business travelers. He went to the airport and waited in line because he knew that if he could create an environment for these people that was tailored to their needs, he would be well compensated.

That cab driver gave himself an edge. He specialized in knowing the needs of a very specific segment of the market. And it paid off.

Set Yourself Apart for Success

A key element of success is finding something that you or your business can be good at. They say, "Dig where the ground is softest," so you start with your natural talent or your company's natural edge. Then, like the cab driver, you leverage that natural ability in your favor.

You specialize.

The "edge" in the specific edge is connected to competition. To have an edge, your performance needs to be superior to your competitors. To have an edge, you need to develop a competitive advantage—a point of differentiation. Specialization gives you that competitive advantage.

Success hinges on setting yourself apart from the crowd in a way that is relevant and compelling. That doesn't mean you have to be the best at everything. It means you have to differentiate yourself from others in a very specific way. For instance, one very effective way to set yourself apart is to understand the needs of your customers better than anyone else. When you do that, people empower you to achieve success by giving you their trust and their business.

Specialization has found its way into a number of areas. Take sports as an example. When you played football as a little kid, you ran all over the field filling any role on the team that you wanted. Offense, defense, both; it didn't matter. Even professional football was like that when it started.

Now look at a professional, modern-day football team. Every person on that team is specialized. You have a quarterback, you have running backs, you have a center. You have an offensive line and a defensive line. You have special teams who just do the kick-offs, punts, and field goals. I once worked out at the New York Giants' training center. While I was there, I saw that each group of specialists on that football team had its own meeting room with its own coaches.

That specialization made each person on the team more valuable, and the whole team was more effective as a result.

The same thing is true with doctors. When you go to the doctor, you might start with your general practitioner. But if you have a serious problem, you go to a specialist who focuses on the kind of ailment you're dealing with. The more specialized the doctor is, the more comfortable you'll feel.

The benefits of specialization are unmatched. When you become an expert in something, your value skyrockets. You're not just providing a service or a product anymore. You're on a whole new level—one where you can respond much better to the needs of the people you're working with or serving.

In fact, at the highest level of specialization, you can do more than respond to those needs: you can anticipate them. You've dealt with a situation, a business, or an issue so many times that you already know what the client is going to ask. You can provide answers to questions that they haven't even thought of asking yet. I'll show you the secrets to this level of specialization in chapter 8.

When you specialize, you understand your customers' strengths and weaknesses. You also understand what is happening in the industry. You know your competition and what that competition is doing to take away your business. Specializing gives you the opportunity to understand the needs of your customers better than anyone else.

Specialization makes you an invaluable asset. It gives you a competitive advantage that will launch you to new levels of success.

To specialize successfully, you need to identify your unique abilities on an individual and a business level, and you need to hone those abilities until you are the best in your field.

Identify Your Specialization: Individual

Where does specialization start? How do you know what you should specialize in?

The best way to identify your specialization is to look at your experiences for clues. There are things you enjoy doing, and things you don't. There are things you're naturally good at, and there are things you don't take to very well. Some people are creative. Some are good at math and science. Everyone has a unique range of natural abilities.

The older you get, the easier it becomes to figure out what your specialization should be, because you've had more experiences. You've been to some different schools. You've had some different jobs. You can think back on those things and pinpoint which areas you liked the best.

So figure out what your strengths are. Maybe you're a great athlete. Maybe you're terrific with people. Maybe you're the funniest person in the room. Identify the things you're good at and enjoy. Then use them to determine a very specific direction for your career.

Define Your Specialization Goals

Once you know where your natural inclinations lie, you can't just stop there. The next step is to define your ideal area of success in a very specific way.

For example, I never said that I wanted to be a "great athlete." I was very specific. I wanted to achieve a level of physical fitness that would allow me to compete in the Ironman World Championship, and I had exact goals for swimming, biking, and running.

When you're an entrepreneur trying to differentiate yourself in the marketplace, you need a competitive advantage. The most powerful way to create that is to be exceptionally good at something very specific. Define what that something is going to be. When you've done that, you're ready to take the next step.

Your Three Unique Attributes

The easiest way to set yourself apart in a large marketplace is to find three things that you're really good at.

Why three things? Because too many people and companies out there can claim to be good at one thing. But at the convergence of your three unique attributes, you are more than just a good specialist.

You are a unique specialist.

The Ironman triathlon is a great example of this. I was a pretty good runner, an above-average swimmer, and a weekend bike rider. But I wasn't so good at any one of them that I could've stood out. When I combined running, swimming, and biking into a long-distance event, however, I excelled.

The same concept was true of my business career. When I became a consultant, I had twenty-eight years of experience in marketing strategies, and I knew that area well. But other consultants have strong marketing experience, too. I set myself apart from the competition by combining my marketing experience with two other attributes: significant sales experience and experience working at a major professional services firm. I knew the marketing and sales sides of professional services, and that gave me a specific edge.

My clients have had similar success with this strategy. For example, one person who works with me is a financial planner. She tailored her practice to serve women who had obtained great wealth through divorce court. These women had never worried about managing finances before. Their ex-husbands had always taken care of it.

So my client leveraged her three unique attributes. She was a great financial planner with twenty-five years of experience and an MBA; she had detailed knowledge of managing the estates of divorcees; and the fact that she was a woman made it easy for her to connect with her target group. She understood what her clients wanted and she was able to provide it. More than that, she could anticipate the problems that her clients didn't even know they had before they ever asked her. That's the power of being specific.

One great talent may not differentiate you. But when you combine three unique talents, you can really stand apart from the competition.

Identify Your Specialization: Business

If you're running or leading a business, the same rule about specialization applies: you need to have a specific edge. That means finding your niche, focusing on your core audience, and setting yourself apart so that you can attract talent, raise money, and leverage expertise.

Everyone in business knows about the big names—your Ford Motors, your McDonalds. But how do really big companies become really big companies in the first place? They weren't born giants.

They started out by specializing.

When Henry Ford started the Ford Motor Company, he made one product. That product was a car. This was back when the roads were dominated by horse-drawn buggies. If you wanted a car, you had to order one custom made.

Ford came in and said, "You can have any car you want, as long as you want it black." The car he offered was mass produced, and it cost significantly less than a customized car. His specific edge was a "horseless carriage" at a great price that was available for purchase right now. The rest is history.

The same thing happened with McDonald's. It started as a couple of hamburger stands that produced one meal: a hamburger or cheeseburger with French fries and a soft drink. When Ray Kroc bought the business off of the McDonald brothers in 1955, the fast food chain exploded across the nation.

Today McDonald's has expanded its menu to include breakfast, salads, chicken nuggets, milkshakes, and a host of other items. But to this day, when you think of McDonald's, what do you think of? You think of a hamburger, fries, and a soft drink.

Even though companies like Ford Motors and McDonald's are huge now, they got where they are because they focused on something very specific to start with.

So if you're a business trying to compete with the giants of the industry, what do you do? You do what they did. You specialize in a defined area. You create a specific edge for yourself by responding to the needs of your small target audience better than anyone who is focused on the masses ever could.

When you're building a business, you don't have the same resources that huge companies like Ford Motors and McDonald's have. You don't have the same type of product development, or the same number of people, or as much capital. You're an underdog, and the most effective way for you to compete is to focus the resources you do have on something specific.

Chobani Greek Yogurt was started in 2005 by Hamdi Ulukaya, a Turkish immigrant who bought an old Kraft Foods plant in New Berlin, New York. He didn't try to create a wide range of dairy products. Ulukaya took on the dairy industry with a yogurt that was made only with natural ingredients, contained real fruit, had twice as much protein as the competition, and did not use gelatin as a thickener. In other words, he specialized big time.

Six years later, his company was the number-one yogurt brand in the United States.

Find a hallmark that sets you apart from the big guys. Dramatically exceed expectations in that one area. That's how you compete at a high level with a fraction of the resources.

That's the power of a specific edge.

Focus on Your Core Audience

To specialize in business, you have to understand your target audience. You can't sell all things to all people. So you have to consider this: How are your unique attributes appealing to your niche market?

Trader Joe's is a business that does this very well. This is a store that carries one type of ketchup and four types of almond butter. That's pretty much the opposite of most grocery stores. But Trader Joe's isn't trying to be most grocery stores. Its visionaries understand their target audience, and they know that their customers aren't looking for ketchup. They're looking for specialty items. That's why they come in, and the fact that they have four types of almond butter to choose from keeps them coming back.

Affinity Bank in Atlanta is another business that has developed a strong competitive edge by focusing on its core audience. Affinity Bank has to compete with names like Bank of America, Wells Fargo, and Sun Trust, all of which are at least a hundred times its size. But it succeeds because it has a very specific core audience: dentists.

Affinity has developed financial products geared specifically toward serving dentists. It has an advisory board of dentists. It collects and shares benchmark data on dental practices. Its loan committees understand the special needs of dentists. When it comes to serving dentists, the larger banks can't compete, and that's how Affinity thrives.

As a professor at Georgia State University, I have my students create a marketing plan for a business of their choice. One year, a male student decided that he was going to write one of these plans for the Hooters in downtown Atlanta. His idea was to extend the restaurant's target audience to appeal to more people—specifically, to families. He wanted to add a children's menu and open up a kids' room upstairs.

But Hooters has been very successful because of its specialized appeal to males ages twenty to forty-nine. That's why it has televisions all over the place and waitresses in revealing outfits.

So I said to my student, "Okay, let's think about your idea. First, what kinds of parents would want to bring their kids into a downtown Hooters? And second, even if the plan was successful and you were able to attract a whole bunch of families with kids, what would that do to the core audience of the business?"

My point was not that my student should exclude children from Hooters. It was that he'd better not invest marketing dollars trying to bring them in. Not when those dollars could get a much bigger return if they were directed at the core audience.

You can't be all things to all people. If you try to do that, you will end up diluting your message, and you will lose the people you set out to serve in the first place.

Never spread your net so wide that you lose sight of your core audience. Focus on better understanding your ideal customer. When you better understand your customers, you build on your competitive advantage. That's a key element of making specialization work.

Go the Distance to Get the Edge

Once you decide to specialize in something, your specific edge doesn't happen overnight. It takes practice, practice, and more practice to become the best at what you do. That's why it's so important to really enjoy what you decide to specialize in. If you're going to devote this kind of time to it, it had better be something you love to do.

When I started training for the Ironman triathlon, I was a strong runner, a pretty good biker, and a weak swimmer. I liked to do all of those things and I had some talent for each of them. But to be successful in the triathlon, I had to focus on developing my skills. I worked with a coach to improve my swimming. I went the extra mile, and I got the training I needed to give myself an edge in the competition.

The taxi driver who specialized in serving businesspeople did the same thing. He knew that he would be well compensated if he could create a peaceful environment in his cab, so he went the distance to figure out how to do that. He probably experimented with different kinds of music. He invested in putting a couple of really nice speakers in the back of his cab.

He put a lot of effort into understanding his customers, and that paid off.

I am the marketing speaker at the National Association of Convenience Stores' school for building food service. In 2013, I spoke at a class where two of the attendees weren't from the convenience-store industry. They supplied the products that convenience stores buy. They attended that class specifically to understand how their customers were trying to grow their food service businesses, because they knew that it would put them in a better position to help those customers by recommending new ideas.

They were setting themselves up to know their customers better, to the point where they'd be able to anticipate their customers' needs. That's the kind of knowledge that gives you a specific edge.

Evolving Specializations

Your specializations will evolve with the times, and they will be driven by the opportunities in your market. Always be on the lookout for opportunities that relate to technology and social media trends, your passion for your work, and your natural abilities.

Technology and Social Media Trends

Technology is a hot area, and you have to be opportunistic where it's concerned.

Many young people have launched rapid career paths by specializing in new technology. They have developed in-depth expertise in industries that did not even exist five years ago. Social media, Facebook advertising, search engine optimization, and app development for mobile devices are all examples of growing fields that offer exciting opportunities in technology.

You don't need to understand all the inner workings of technology to benefit from it, either. In the 1970s, a young lawyer by the name of John Yates saw how computers were changing the way that businesses operated. And he saw how those changes would fit into the legal field. Intellectual capital, strategic partnerships, raising capital—all of these things were going to become big legal issues, and he anticipated that.

So John decided to specialize in that industry. He became an expert on legal issues related to technology. Today, John's firm—Morris, Manning & Martin—is the leading law firm for technology companies in the southeastern United States.

Technology plays a huge role in today's global marketplace. Healthcare, social media, alternative energy sources—whatever field you're in, technology is there. When you take advantage of it, you capitalize on an opportunity to hone your specialization. And you drive yourself further down the path to success.

Your Passion

Always focus on the things that you're passionate about. When you love to do something, you are more committed, more successful, and happier.

Passion is often overlooked when it comes to achieving success as an entrepreneur. But people who do what they love are more successful than people who do what they do purely for the economic benefit.

That means you need to take stock of what you're doing and why you're doing it. If you're not passionate about the things on your schedule, reinvent yourself. Find that passion, and follow it as it changes. Your specialization should go where your passion goes.

Your Natural Abilities

As you mature, your natural abilities change. You develop some new ones and you lose some old ones. To keep from getting stuck on those changes, you have to adjust. You have to embrace the new opportunities and let go of the old ones. You have to be willing to develop new skills.

If you try to hold on to the old and the new at the same time, you will lose your edge as a specialist.

As your opportunities change and your passion evolves, expand and reinvent your skills to keep up with them. The challenge here is staying current enough to recognize a great opportunity when you see it. Then you have to be nimble enough to act on it.

In the 1980s, I was approached by a headhunter who asked me to consider taking the second-highest position in marketing at a software company in Seattle. At the time, I was only willing to consider the chief marketing officer position. I wasn't interested in working for someone else.

That "someone else" turned out to be Steve Ballmer, and the company was Microsoft. I let my ego get in the way, and I missed a great opportunity because I couldn't recognize it.

Stay current in your area of expertise by reading blogs and publications related to your field. Attend conferences. Go to networking events. Follow the futurists, and always try to understand the implications and unintended consequences of what they are predicting.

Cutting-Edge Success

Specialization gives you a critical edge as an entrepreneur. As a specialist, you have the tools and the finely honed talent to come in a cut above your competition.

When you specialize, you outsmart your competition. You understand your very specific area of expertise better than anyone. That opens the door for you to better serve your customers with products or services that match their specific needs. You gain an advantage over your competition that moves you one step closer to your vision.

But having the tools is one thing, and using them to achieve your long-term goals is another. Raw talent isn't enough, even when it's specialized. Putting in the effort to hone your specific edge is what wins the day.

The next key principle on the journey to success is discipline.

▲

CHAPTER THREE
Gain The Edge Through Discipline

With self-discipline most anything is possible.

THEODORE ROOSEVELT

Discipline behind the Scenes: Hines Ward

One of the most successful football players of the early 2000s was Hines Ward. Ward played wide receiver for the Pittsburgh Steelers for fourteen years. During his time with the Steelers, the team won two Super Bowls, and Ward was named Most Valuable Player of Super Bowl XL.

But Hines Ward didn't stop there. In 2011, he won the hit national television competition *Dancing with the Stars*. Then he competed in the Ironman World Championship.

Anybody looking at this man thinks, "Wow, he was born with a huge amount of talent."

But what people don't see is the amount of practice that Ward put into every one of those achievements. This is a man who trained to go to training camp when he signed on with the Steelers. Before he set foot on the *Dancing with the Stars* stage, he spent eight hours a day for eleven weeks learning how to dance.

Ward and I trained together for the Ironman World Championship. I took him on his first hundred-mile bike ride in the north Georgia mountains. I saw firsthand the kind of dedication he put into his dreams.

No matter what goal he took on, Hines Ward trained constantly. He always found ways to improve.

He is the emblem of how discipline leads to success.

Defining Discipline

What is discipline? Why is it such a critical part of success?

Discipline is related to the development of your specific edge. In a nutshell, it's about getting better. It's about looking for improvement, tracking improvement, and trying out new ideas for improvement.

Discipline hones your edge constantly so that you can overcome obstacles and stay ahead of the competition. Like Hines Ward, disciplined people always find ways to outsmart their competitors, build their talents, and compete at a higher level.

Chapter 2 was about choosing your specialization. Discipline is the focus you place on that specialization to hone it into a formidable edge. It's about weaving that focus into the fabric of everything you do in your career or your business. That might mean customer relations. It might mean product development. It might be communications and promotions. It might relate to the whole culture.

Whatever you're developing, discipline is the force that turns your goals into successful realities.

Success isn't easy. Overcoming obstacles is a challenge for anybody. You have to make sacrifices. If you're an athlete, that means giving up some "fun foods" so that your body gets ideal nutrition. If you're a businessperson, it might mean putting in long hours or being on the road a lot. And at some point, it will probably mean overcoming setbacks to keep moving forward.

We often look at someone who's successful, like Hines Ward, and think, "That guy is just incredibly talented. He's just incredibly lucky. He's just incredibly blessed to have the skills that he has. He was born with a magic touch, and that's why he's a superstar."

We're shocked when we learn that that isn't usually the case. Usually, the Hines Wards of the world got where they are because they had enough discipline to keep themselves focused on their goals.

Talent wasn't the key to their success. Discipline was.

The Importance of Practice

It's easy to see how practice benefits people in the sports world. We've developed a whole industry around it. We have machines, coaches, training programs, and nutrition plans. If you don't practice, you're not going to win.

But how much do people practice in the business world? How many executives have coaches? How many of them are constantly honing their people-management skills? How many mentors do they have to keep them learning and growing stronger?

The power of practice in business is completely underestimated. When I worked with a major accounting firm, I always marveled at the way we handled our presentations to new clients. We'd put huge amounts of time and energy into researching and developing those presentations, but we almost never scheduled time to practice them ahead of time.

We never ran through the finished product to make sure that the message came across clearly. The practice part of the presentation usually happened in the car on the way to see the client. If we rode in separate cars, then we practiced in the client's waiting room, assuming the client wasn't already waiting to see us when we arrived.

Without practice, success is usually out of reach. And the determination to practice comes from one thing: discipline. True discipline involves showing up, monitoring your performance, and getting feedback.

The Three Keystones of Discipline

Discipline is about getting better. You get better by targeting specific areas of yourself or your business that need improvement. When it comes to discipline, there are three keystones that demand your focus. You have to show up. You have to monitor your performance. And you have to get feedback and act on that good advice to continuously improve yourself.

Show Up

Discipline starts with showing up, even when you don't want to.

When I trained for Ironman, I woke up at five o'clock every morning to train. Even when it was cold. Even when it was raining. There were plenty of mornings when I would just as soon have stayed in my warm bed, but I was competing at a level that demanded that I show up. I was competing at a level that demanded discipline.

You need to have the discipline to follow through with your goals. There may not be anything in it for you in the short term, but you need to stick with it anyway. You need to keep your focus on your long-term vision. And you need to push through the obstacles to get to where you want to go. When you face competitive pressure, miss key components, misjudge the competition, or fail to complete a crucial step, it's your discipline that will put you back on track.

When I lived in Chicago, I knew one of the best amateur golfers in the area: Joel Hirsch. Everyone was amazed by how well Joel played golf. But he didn't play well because he was born talented. Every time I went by the golf course, Joel was out there, practicing his putt or his swing. He practiced more than anyone I knew.

Joel didn't play well because he was born a natural golfer. He played well because he was out on the course all the time. He played well because he showed up.

Practicing your putt is one thing. Practicing your putt one hundred times every day is discipline.

Without discipline, you are going to have a hard time showing up. And without showing up, you're much less likely to achieve success.

Monitor Performance

The second keystone of discipline is monitoring your performance. This is even more important than showing up. You have to track your results to see how you're doing.

When you track your results, you have a guideline for progress. You can see where you've been, you can see where you're going, and you can project how much longer it will take to reach your goal. You can identify your weak links and eliminate them. You can also make adjustments to help you become more efficient.

Many people don't want to bother keeping track of the details. That's why monitoring performance takes discipline. Tracking your progress doesn't have much of a short-term benefit, but the long-term benefits are enormous. When you track your performance, you empower yourself to identify problem areas and to recognize and reward improvement.

As an athlete, you constantly track your performance. You time yourself and you record those numbers. You track your speed and your distance as you run, bike, and swim. You track your heart rate from week to week. Then you use that data and more to calculate your rate of improvement. Where are you getting stronger? Where are you still weak? At this pace, will you reach your goal fast enough? What changes do you need to make to your routine?

The same rule is true in business. When you monitor your performance, you get better results. Maybe you're a salesperson. One of the key things you'd track is your close rate; the percentage of qualified prospects you are able to convert into customers. A low close rate tells you one of two things. Either you're doing a poor job screening for qualified prospects, or your sales process needs to be improved.

So you ask yourself: How many people are you talking to, and how many of those people convert to sales? What percent of the people who visit your store or come to your website actually buy a product or service? What are the numbers?

Then you use those numbers to improve. What areas of your business are weak? What areas are strong? When you uncover those weak spots by examining the facts, you can work to improve your result.

Plenty of companies collect data from comment cards. But how disciplined are they with those cards once they get them? Do they actually read the feedback they're getting? And do they have a system in place to correct the problems they find? Without the discipline to use the feedback, the feedback itself is useless.

One great example of a company that does wonders with feedback is Patagonia. Patagonia is a clothing manufacturer that serves serious skiers and climbers. It constantly sends out ambassadors to solicit feedback from its customers. Then it uses that feedback to create products that address its clients' very specific needs.

One of those products is the Patagonia ice-climber jacket. Ice climbers have their arms up in the air constantly. When water runs down the ice, it trickles down their arms and into their jackets. Patagonia makes a jacket with extra-long sleeves and tight wrist cuffs to eliminate that problem. The company got that idea from its professional ice-climber ambassador, and Patagonia now has an advantage over its competitors in that very specific market.

Compiling a lot of data on a daily basis can get tedious. Again, that's where discipline comes in. Tracking your progress is a key part of making sure that you are constantly improving and getting closer to the goal. You have to have the discipline to be quantitative about your actions.

You have to have the discipline to track results.

Get Feedback and Continuously Improve

The third keystone of discipline is getting feedback and using it to continuously improve.

To improve, you need to get feedback from others about how you're doing. That feedback might come from a coach, a peer review, or a colleague. Whatever the case, quality advice gets you thinking about improvement in new ways.

But "thinking" isn't enough. Good feedback is pointless unless you act on it. The other half of the deal is taking the suggestions you get and using them to make positive changes. Ask yourself what you have to do to turn a good idea into an effective reality. Be specific. Then don't give up until you can actually see the improvement you were going for.

When I trained for Ironman, I monitored my performance and found that biking was the weak link in my athletic skills. I knew I had to focus on improving that specific area. So I hired a coach to give me advice. Then I took that advice and started using it in my routines. When I did those two things, my biking skills quickly improved.

The same concept applies to business. When you find your weak spot, the best way to improve it is to bring in someone who has experience in that area.

Hang around with people who are on a journey that is similar to yours. In sports, that means connecting with others who are training for the same goal. When you find those people, you share your best practice strategies, you share your wins, and you help each other overcome setbacks. You make yourself get out of bed in the morning because you know that someone is out there waiting for you to show up for training. You listen to their advice, and you offer yours when they ask for it.

In business, getting and using feedback might mean joining a Professional Experts Group (PEG) or becoming part of a mastermind group like Young Presidents' Organization, Vistage, or Entrepreneurs' Organization. It might mean bringing in a mentor or inviting a speaker to talk to your group. Always surround yourself with people whose feedback you can use to push yourself toward continuous improvement.

Discipline is about getting better, and you get better by showing up, monitoring your performance, and getting and using advice from a quality source. When you do these things, you develop a more powerful message. You understand your customers and are better able to cater to their needs. You truly excel in your chosen specialization.

You achieve success.

The Edge of Discipline

As I wrote this chapter on discipline, I reluctantly realized that I myself wasn't following one part of the plan: I was training for Ironman, and I wasn't keeping track of my training results. I felt like too much structure would take the fun out of it. I didn't want to live life like a machine. But I knew I needed to keep some kind of structure in place in order to improve.

So I added that structure, but I also gave myself some freedom to adjust my workout within certain guidelines. I substituted a great bike ride for a long run when I felt like it, then made up the run on another day. I kept track of my daily effort by monitoring time, distance, speed, and heart rate.

My discipline was back. And so was my ongoing improvement as an athlete.

Discipline is an enormous factor in honing your specific edge. It can be the difference between a dream that becomes reality and a dream that remains unattainable. Even though it is sometimes one of the hardest things to do, it's also one of the things that you have the most control over. You can control your level of commitment. You can control your self-motivation. And you can use those things to get you where you want to go in the long term.

But discipline isn't the only principle that factors into developing your edge. Another critical part of that is endurance—the next step on the path to success.

A winner has more than just a vision of success. A winner continues to push forward through the obstacles that stand between him or her and that vision.

MIKE WIEN

▲

CHAPTER FOUR

Endure To Succeed

Success is the ability to go from failure to failure
without losing your enthusiasm.

WINSTON CHURCHILL

Frito-Lay: Bust to Blockbuster

I had been at Frito-Lay for only five years when I got my first big break. I was asked to launch the company's brand-new product: Fantastix.

Frito-Lay gave me $29 million to develop the plan to roll out Fantastix, a new potato-based product in the shape of a French fry. The roll out was nationwide. We launched the brand and expanded production to thirty plants across the country over a three-week period. We wanted to take advantage of national TV advertising in tandem with the launch.

Well, the marketing did exactly what it was supposed to do. It drove huge demand for the trial of the product.

And that resulted in the biggest disaster that Frito-Lay had ever seen.

Fantastix tasted great in the pre-launch market, when the product was manufactured in a test kitchen with a bunch of PhDs watching over the line. But when we tried to produce it under normal factory conditions, it became inedible. Our successful marketing turned out to be the kiss of death for the brand.

We pulled the product off the shelves six weeks after its introduction.

Not long after that fiasco, I was sitting in my office when my secretary told me I had a phone call from the administrative assistant for Senior Vice President of Marketing and Sales Bill Korn. "Mr. Korn wants to see you in his office," she said.

I remember that moment vividly. I put on my suit jacket. I looked around my office at the couple of books on the desk, the potted plant, the picture of my wife.

This is the part where I get my pink slip, I thought.

When I got to Bill Korn's office, he sat me down and said, "Well Mike, Fantastix didn't do so well."

I was tempted to say something in my defense. But I kept my mouth shut.

"It's too bad we had to pull it off the market," he went on. "Anyway, I called you in because I want to give you another new product to introduce."

I stared at him. I wasn't sure I'd heard the words correctly. Was he nuts? I couldn't stop myself. "What are you thinking?" I blurted. "I just rolled out the biggest turkey that Frito-Lay has ever seen. I have no credibility in the organization. And you want me to launch another one?"

Bill Korn looked me dead in the eye and said, "Mike, we just spent $29 million training you. That was one heck of a learning experience. But now you know what you need to know. You learned what we need to do differently, because you were in the middle of it. The entire organization is snake-bit about launching another product right now. You understand the issues and concerns better than anyone. That makes you the ideal person to roll this out."

So I accepted the task. I used what I had learned from the Fantastix disaster, and I launched the next product for Frito-Lay.

That product was Tostitos. And it was the most successful food brand introduced in the 1970s.

What Is Endurance?

Like discipline, endurance is a key part of developing your specific edge. Over the long term, you're going to have setbacks like my Fantastix experience. You're going to miscalculate. Your competitor is going to outsmart you. Every person and every organization has to deal with adversity. But only those who persevere and stay focused on their visions achieve success in the long term.

Endurance is about developing the ability to overcome adversity. It's about having the willpower to push past obstacles and keep on marching forward toward your goal.

Endurance can mean the difference between success and failure. In fact, success is built on failure—specifically, on the ability to overcome it. All too often, you put your plans in place, you train hard, and something comes up to sabotage you. That's when endurance kicks in. The people who endure are the ones who overcome those obstacles to reach success. They keep building the relationship. They keep moving forward. And eventually they get where they want to go.

Ironman is a great example of endurance. Yes, you need to develop some good athletic skills, but the activities themselves are not what the competition is about. The competition is about being able to perform at a very high level for eight to seventeen hours straight. It's about overcoming the adversity that is thrown at you, whether that's a strong headwind, dehydration, leg cramps, or heat coming off of volcanic rock.

Ironman is about endurance.

Endurance plays an equally big role in the business world. When most individuals or companies start out, they face a ton of obstacles. The difference between the people who fail and the ones who succeed is that the ones who succeed know how to overcome those obstacles. They know how to face the setback, learn from the experience, and continue moving forward anyway.

They know how to endure.

I break endurance down into three key parts: keeping your eye on the long term instead of the short term, overcoming obstacles, and avoiding burnout.

Long Term versus Short Term

Success is about the long term. Focusing only on short-term rewards is not going to help you reach your dreams. All too often, short-term goals are not consistent with long-term objectives.

People in our society are increasingly looking for instant gratification. The same can be said of companies that focus on quarterly earnings. If they don't see an immediate reward, they move on. Some businesses get caught up in insider trading and other illegal activities. They care more about short-term satisfaction than they do about long-term success.

Even in the sports world, some people try to take shortcuts. They don't want to put the time and development into being the best, so they resort to performance-enhancing drugs. Then they get caught, and their success evaporates. It was never real to begin with.

They try for short-term success. They end up with a long-term disaster.

By and large, really successful companies didn't come from short-term luck. They came from long-term endurance. The people who started them had an idea, and they fought for it. They fought to get that idea on the market. They fought to get the financing they needed. They fought to overcome the obstacles in their paths. Why? Because they had a long-term vision, and that vision kept them moving forward.

Business itself relies on long-term endurance. For instance, successful salespeople aren't usually successful because they walk up to strangers and sell them things on the spot. They're successful because of the relationships they build. They take the time to understand the real needs of their customers, recommend solutions, fill a void, or leverage an opportunity. They have the endurance to develop trust and a good rapport with their clients.

In other words, they don't just go for the low-hanging fruit. They nurture the relationship and harvest the whole tree.

Long-term investors in the stock market also understand the value of endurance. In 2007 when the market collapsed, a lot of people cut and run. But the long-term investors stuck it out. Between 2007 and 2013, the stock market experienced one of the largest increases that the country has seen in a generation. The long-term investors who stayed put reaped the benefits of that.

The business world is packed with successful companies that kept their eyes on the long-term picture.

One of them is Tylenol. In Chicago in the early 1980s, seven people died after taking Tylenol capsules that had been laced with cyanide. That was the kind of scare that could have doomed the company. But Tylenol was in it for the long term. The organization did a national recall of all Tylenol capsules. Every box and bottle of Tylenol came off the shelves. Then the company replaced those old products with a new package that featured three safety seals: one underneath the cap, one on the cap itself, and finally the box.

When Tylenol re-launched its product, its competitors had no safety seals. Other painkillers were unprotected, and the businesses making them couldn't justify replacing all their existing stock just to incorporate similar seals. That gave Tylenol a major competitive advantage that reestablished the brand, which is still going strong today.

Another great example of long-term success is Snapple. Leonard Marsh launched Snapple in the early 1970s. Over the next seventeen years, he grew his beverage business to $24 million. Not great results. Then, between 1989 and 1994, Snapple's growth exploded to $674 million. Those five years were hailed by the world as an overnight success. But it took seventeen years of hard work just to get Snapple to the launching pad before it saw its dramatic growth.

Too often, individuals and businesses alike don't have the foresight to make long-term investments. They overlook the value of endurance in their business plans. They emphasize the short term, where the focus is internal. "How can I make this sale to meet this month's quota? How can I get that bonus to pay for my kid's college tuition?"

The long-term approach, meanwhile, has an external focus. It asks completely different questions. "What products or services best fill the needs of my client? If I don't have those products and services, who can I recommend that does provide them?"

The internal approach might succeed in generating a quick sale. But the long-term external approach generates a customer for life. Endurance is about the external approach.

Endurance is about lifelong success.

Overcome Obstacles

Overcoming obstacles is the cornerstone of endurance. Because that's what endurance is. Endurance is the ability to keep going in the face of obstacles.

Pushing through obstacles can be an enormous challenge. You have to have passion, you have to have discipline, and you have to have faith in your idea. You also have to accept that sometimes the idea won't be the right one, and you have to make the necessary adjustments either to the plan or to your goal.

Obstacles show us what we're made of. You really see how good a person is by the way he or she handles the things that go wrong. For example, US Airways pilot C. B. Sullenberger was just another person who flew jets until January 15, 2009, when birds got sucked into his engines shortly after he took off from LaGuardia Airport in New York. That day, Sullenberger successfully landed his plane in the middle of the Hudson River without his jet engines, saving 155 lives.

Sullenberger was an extraordinary pilot, but nobody knew it until that event took place. Because of the way he handled that crisis, he became a national hero.

One of my favorite examples of endurance is Lee Iacocca, the CEO of Chrysler. When Lee was fired as the president of Ford Motor Company and took over Chrysler in the late 1970s, Chrysler was on the verge of bankruptcy. The obstacles the company faced were staggering. In the face of them, Lee turned that business around. He brought in new talent. He solved problems. He took the company back to basics and kept it moving forward. Chrysler became a very successful car company again. All because Lee Iacocca had endurance.

History is littered with examples like Chrysler. Steven Spielberg was rejected from the University of Southern California film school three times and dropped out of his backup school before becoming one of the most recognized directors in the world. Theodor Seuss Geisel, better known as Dr. Seuss, was rejected by publishers twenty-seven times before he became history's most successful children's book author. Walt Disney was fired by a newspaper for lacking imagination before he created Mickey Mouse. And Oprah Winfrey was fired from her first job in television because she was "unfit for TV."

My experience with Ironman is something similar. There is not an Ironman triathlete in the ranks who doesn't wonder, somewhere around sixty or seventy miles in, what on earth he or she is doing out there. My claim to fame is that I was second in the world in my age group in the Ironman World Championship, but that didn't happen on my first attempt. I competed in eight years of Ironman races and made it to the world championship two other times before I captured that second-place finish.

Endurance goes beyond the physical. It takes emotional endurance to keep moving forward, no matter how much you want to quit. In the end, endurance is mind over matter, all the way to the finish.

Whether you're competing in an Ironman or building a company, obstacles will always get in the way. Success goes to those who develop the ability to get around those obstacles and keep moving forward. Success goes to those with endurance.

Avoid Burnout

Endurance isn't about wielding a vast amount of energy. It's about managing that energy in a way that gets you all the way to your goal. It's about balancing the physical, mental, emotional, and spiritual factors of your life. I talk more about balance in the next chapter.

Without endurance, you run into one of the biggest obstacles to success: burnout.

The most successful Ironman athletes aren't the fastest swimmers, bikers, or runners. They are the people who can combine all of those things and still compete at an above-average level. They're the people who can manage their energy over a long period of time without burning themselves out.

In business, endurance means managing your resources to help you achieve your long-term goals. How often do we put all of our focus on developing a great event to attract clients and prospects, then realize that we don't have any energy left to follow up with the people who came? Endurance translates into staying power that lasts through the whole business cycle.

That's how you avoid burnout. That's how you keep your organization moving toward success.

Endure to the Finish

A winner has more than just a vision of success. A winner continues to push forward through the obstacles that stand between him or her and that vision. Winners bring their whole organization along on the journey, and they stay focused on the goal in spite of all odds.

That's what endurance is really about.

Calvin Coolidge once said, "Nothing in the world can take the place of persistence. Talent will not; nothing is more common than unsuccessful men with talent. Genius will not; unrewarded genius is almost a proverb. Education will not; the world is full of educated derelicts. Persistence and determination alone are omnipotent. The slogan 'Press On!' has solved and always will solve the problems of the human race."

Success is often the result of persistence. It comes from overcoming obstacles and setbacks. When you can stay focused on the end goal in the face of adversity, you have tapped into one of the strongest qualities you have. Endurance is a major asset for keeping that focus intact.

Those who endure are in it for the long term. One key factor that keeps endurance going strong over the weeks, months, and years of working toward a goal is balance. Without balance, endurance becomes impossible, and your specific edge drifts out of reach. That's why balance is the next step on the journey to success.

▲

CHAPTER FIVE
A Balanced Edge

Out of clutter, find simplicity. From disorder, find harmony. In the middle of difficulty lies opportunity.

ALBERT EINSTEIN

Balancing Act

I've heard it said many times that if you want to get something done, ask a busy person.

For me, that busy person is Scott Boylan. Scott is the complex manager for Morgan Stanley in Baltimore. He's also my good friend, Ironman training buddy, and Timex Multisport teammate.

Scott and his wife Joanne have four sons. On top of that, he is responsible for over four hundred people. But he still finds the time to train for an Ironman. He stays active in his church. He's involved in his younger boys' activities, and he skis every chance he gets in the winter.

He has more energy than anyone else I know, and he manages to pack all of that and more into a very exciting, rich, and purposeful life. The perspective he draws from the variety of experiences in his life makes him great in a crisis. It helps him create an environment that people love. It makes people want to follow him. Not because he's a superman. They want to follow him because he's a role model.

Scott lives an exciting life filled with passion, and he never burns out. He's multidimensional and interesting to talk to, something that helps him start new relationships and keep them going. He's so good at keeping everything in perspective that he attracts people who do the same thing.

He understands the power of balance.

Balance: Physical, Mental, Emotional, and Spiritual

You've asked a lot of yourself so far on your journey to success. You've dug deep to connect with a dream that's true to you. You've honed that dream into a specialized focus. You've disciplined yourself to reach new heights in your field, and you've endured tremendous obstacles to keep pushing forward toward your goal. None of that is easy. To keep it all going long term, you need a formidable set of tools waiting in the wings.

The first of those tools is balance.

One of the greatest challenges that goes hand in hand with pushing to build a specific edge is burnout. Balance is key to avoiding that hurdle. It keeps you moving at a steady rate over time. It helps you to keep going in the face of obstacles. It gives you the perspective and the mental agility to stay focused on your ultimate goal. Companies that encourage balance are the ones that experience long-term success.

I divide balance into four parts: physical, mental, emotional, and spiritual.

Ironman embodies balance on each of these levels. Success in an Ironman takes a lot more than being in great physical shape. You have to have all four kinds of balance in place to keep up with the intense level of commitment, as well.

Physical balance is an obvious prerequisite for success in an Ironman. You need to develop strong muscles and proper techniques, such as pedaling on both the upstroke and the downstroke when you're on the bike. Aerobic capacity is critical if you want to put out a significant amount of effort and maintain a steady heart rate at the same time. Physical balance is widely recognized as a must-have for a major sporting event.

But the other three areas are equally vital for success. Mentally, you have to develop the right training program, set the right pace, and manage your nutrition plan. Emotionally, you need to build a strong support network of friends, family, and training partners to support you along the way. And spiritually, you need to appreciate your own ability to compete. You need to have empathy for your competitors. You need to be grateful for the four thousand volunteers standing out there on the side of the road making sure that you have everything you need. You need to be inspired to give something back in return for everything you receive.

In business, not everybody makes a connection between balance and success. But if you aren't physically healthy, how does that impact your energy to conduct business? If you aren't emotionally balanced, how does that affect your ability to make good decisions? And if you aren't spiritually balanced, how does your disconnect from a larger purpose impact the choices you make on a daily basis?

Striking a balance between these four areas—physical, mental, emotional, and spiritual—is a strategy that can affect every aspect of your life and your career. It keeps you going steady no matter what kind of finish line you're aiming to cross.

As individuals, we need to strike balance in our personal lives. As entrepreneurs, we need to make it part of our business culture.

When we fail to do these things, we end up running into the same wall: burnout.

The Cost of Imbalance: Burnout

Burnout is the ultimate cost of neglecting balance. You put so much focus and energy into your area of specialization that you develop a myopic view of the world. You neglect other things that really matter, whether those things are physical, mental, emotional, or spiritual. And before you know what hit you, the excitement and the passion you had for your goal evaporates.

Burnout comes with serious consequences. Too many triathletes have dropped out of the sport or, worse, have made their wives or husbands into Ironman widows or widowers. Too many business-people sacrifice everything for their jobs: their health, their families, their friends, and ultimately their sense of purpose. Then they wake up one morning and wonder, "What was it all for?"

The two big culprits of imbalance are being a workaholic and feeding bad habits.

Workaholic

Workaholics are some of the most imbalanced people I know. And that imbalance has some truly negative effects on their lives.

Workaholics have trouble managing others, because they expect everyone else to live up to their own unhealthy work levels. They push their people, and they burn out their teams. They have a hard time holding on to the best and the brightest, who want balanced work environments.

Workaholics endanger the personal aspects of their lives as well. They lose contact with their families. They don't maintain their friendships. Their health deteriorates. They forget to celebrate their journeys because they're so focused on the end result.

They can't remember why they wanted to reach their goals in the first place, because they've lost their sense of purpose.

Bad Habits

People also swing out of balance when they let themselves develop bad habits. They come up with excuses to justify those habits so that they don't have to face and correct the problem. They have an excuse for why they aren't eating well, why they aren't getting enough sleep, why they can't find time to exercise. And the bad habits just keep going.

Bad habits chip away at your balance. They drain your energy and your focus. When you let yourself get away with them, it has real consequences in your daily life. You can't think clearly. You can't solve problems.

You can't keep moving forward toward your goal.

Create Balance

Creating balance not only helps you complete your journey, it also makes the journey itself more enjoyable. When you're balanced, you're healthier and you nurture strong relationships. Keeping up an interest in other things stimulates your creativity for your specific edge. Balance keeps you nimble. It helps you anticipate and adjust to change. All of this is critical to success. But how do you create balance when all the odds are stacked against you?

Even when the situation is tough, you have to find a way to use what you have.

For example, some people choose to skip their vacation time because they think they're irreplaceable, or they think it will make them look like better employees. But I've worked for a lot of companies, and I've never heard anyone say, "Hey look, this is Joe. He's never taken a day of vacation. We'd never last a day if he left us. What a great employee, congratulations." And I've never seen anyone lose his or her job for taking vacation days, either.

The responsibility falls to you. You need to recognize that if you don't take those vacation days, you're going to work yourself to death. You're going to make yourself into a less productive employee.

You need to understand the value of balance when it comes to producing value. Yes, you have to work hard, but you have to schedule downtime, too. If you're a leader, you have to make yourself a role model for everyone in your organization. The higher up you go in a company, the more you are valued for your mind over your physical activities. People who live balanced lives develop broader perspectives. They set aside time to challenge their brains on multiple levels. That makes them better thinkers who can add greater value to their companies.

It's not just about working hard. It's about working at your highest level of value. And that can only be achieved through living a balanced life.

One client of mine is an accountant. From January to March every year, there is no room in his life for balance. He is completely focused on sleeping, eating, and working. So what does balance mean for him?

In that kind of situation, it's a question of the long-term picture. If you know that you're going to be out of balance the first three months of the year, you'd better make sure that you're exceptionally balanced for the other nine months. You'd better be focused on your health, your family, and your community while you can. The balance you create in those nine months is where you're going to draw the strength you need to survive the other three.

Balance may not always be a day-to-day or even a week-to-week event. But when you learn to follow it as a long-term strategy, you gain the endurance to achieve your dreams.

A Culture of Balance

If you lead an organization, balance works on two levels. You need to model it yourself, and you need to promote it in your company culture. A company culture of balance is key to business success.

A culture of balance attracts people who aren't just in it for the paycheck. These are people who are passionate about their careers. They're people who are in it for the long haul. They're people who are committed to living exciting lives.

These are the people you want on your team.

The new business paradigm that is emerging puts a lot of value on balanced company culture. The nature of the workforce is changing. Many baby boomers who held senior positions are leaving those roles. Companies are looking to replace them with the best and brightest of the new generation.

But the new generation has different values than their parents did. The new generation isn't looking to show up at nine in the morning, leave at five in the afternoon, and get their gold watches for being loyal to the company after forty years. People in their thirties are much more focused on making a positive impact in the world. They're more sensitive about their overall quality of life. They're not loyal to a specific company, but they're loyal to ideas. They're loyal to organizations where they can use those ideas to make a difference.

For the new generation, balance is a priority. That means the companies that will attract and retain the best new talent are the companies that likewise develop a culture of balance.

Some companies put real energy into creating a balanced culture. Others just give the concept lip service. You can't hold a company picnic once a year for your employees and their families and then pretend that you support a healthy work-life balance.

You have to make a real commitment.

A true culture of balance promotes physical, mental, emotional, and spiritual balance among the individuals in an organization. It encourages employees to cultivate balance in their personal lives, and it does that in a wide range of ways.

Some companies offer health clubs or wellness programs to their employees. Some offer massages. Some make sure that their employees aren't working too many hours. I know of a consulting firm where the company contacts an employee's immediate supervisor if that individual's hours go up too high, just to make sure that the person in question isn't burning out the team.

There are endless ways to create a culture of balance in your organization. You can offer sabbaticals. You can introduce family counseling programs. Some companies have created a policy where employees who need to travel only do so Monday through Thursday. That allows them to be at home with their families four nights a week.

Some companies also encourage their employees to give back to the community. They give them opportunities to serve on a not-for-profit board, to attend a volunteer day, to get out and be active in their neighborhoods or in their houses of worship. All of these things support spiritual balance. The employees who participate in them not only feel productive, they feel good about themselves as well.

The point of a balanced culture is to make sure that your employees stay healthy. You want them to develop relationships and friendships, to give back to the community, to get the training they want in order to grow in their roles.

You want to empower them to live a balanced lifestyle.

When you empower your employees to live balanced lives, the benefits are enormous. You will attract and retain the best and the brightest of the incoming generation. You will be competitive as you move toward the future. You will have people who bring discipline, intelligence, excitement, and endurance to your big picture and your bottom line.

Best of all, you will have a team of people who live exciting, multidimensional lives. They will be more creative, more motivated, and more positive about their jobs, their coworkers, and their daily experiences. They will have broader perspectives that help them identify opportunities and overcome setbacks. They will become magnets that attract other high-talent individuals, and their enthusiasm will be infectious.

They will be the team you need to achieve long-term success.

Balance Your Relationships

Balance is also critical when it comes to developing relationships. In business, that means building trust with colleagues and clients. The best way to do that isn't to talk about business itself.

The best way to do that is to find common ground beyond the business sphere.

That's where a multidimensional life becomes such a critical tool. When you have multiple interests, you can create multiple points of connection with the people you want to build relationships with. They help you connect with others on a personal level so that you can express an interest in someone else beyond, "What can you do for me today?"

When you let people know that you see them as more than just a source of revenue, you earn trust. When you earn trust, you earn business.

Whenever I meet someone for the first time, I always try to make a personal connection before I get into business. If the other person is a triathlete or a runner, I'm home free—we'll be best friends in minutes. The common connections, stories, and friends that come out of that mutual interest give us a bond right away.

The connections you can make with other people are limitless. You can find them in the cities where you have both lived, in your kids, in your volunteer work, in your alma mater, or in your favorite hobby. And even if you don't find a connection in any of those, you can still relate to someone on a personal level just by showing an interest in the things that matter to them.

I once asked a new client about his hobbies and he said, "I'm a train watcher." I didn't believe him for a minute, but it was true. It turns out that a whole lot of people enjoy watching trains and identifying the different engines as they motor by. Folkston, a small town in southern Georgia, has even made a tourist attraction out of it. All Florida-bound trains traveling from forty-seven states have to come through this train-track artery. For train watchers, it's just pure, uninterrupted joy.

I didn't know anything about watching trains. But the next time I was in Jacksonville, Florida, I drove over to that town in Georgia and sat on the viewing platform for an hour. Then I bought a train hat from the gift shop and gave it to my client for the holidays.

That hat didn't cost me much, but it sent a powerful message to my client. It told him that I cared about him as a person, not just as a revenue source.

He continues to be a great client and referral source for my business to this day.

Balance Yourself

There's a lot to be said about a work environment that has a balanced culture. But at the end of the day, there is only one person who can really bring balance to your life.

That person is you.

You are responsible for cultivating the balance you need to achieve your dreams and live life with purpose. You can do it with the help of your company, or you can do it in spite of all odds. Like the triathlete who controls how much effort he or she is expending on each leg of the race, you are the one who monitors how much of your energy goes to the physical, mental, emotional, and spiritual aspects of your life.

Balance is a critical value on the journey to success. But it isn't the only tool you have to help you achieve your specific edge. Next, let's take a look at the second tool in your kit: attitude.

A positive environment inspires people to find solutions to problems instead of excuses to slow down progress.

MIKE WIEN

▲

CHAPTER SIX
Use Attitude To Create An Edge

---

*We can complain because rose bushes have thorns, or
rejoice because thorn bushes have roses.*

ABRAHAM LINCOLN

Column G

I once mentored a man named Dick Jones, whose goal was to
run the Boston Marathon. I've mentored some pretty incredible
people. But let me tell you, Dick was meticulous.

He tracked absolutely everything, and he recorded the data in a
chart. That chart had columns labeled all the way up to column
G. One column was for distance. One column was for heart rate.
One column was for weather. Every possible detail that you can
record when you're training for a marathon was somewhere on
Dick's chart.

One day, Dick gave me the chart and asked me what I thought of
it. I looked over each of the columns. A, B, C, D . . . everything
seemed to be in order. Then I got to column G.

Column G was full of reasons that Dick's run hadn't been perfect
that day. The weather was bad. His muscles needed to recuperate
from yesterday's workout. A big deadline was looming at work and

he had to skip running altogether. Column G didn't serve a useful purpose like its six neighbors.

Column G was a list of excuses.

I looked at Dick and said, "I really appreciate all the tracking you've done here. But column G is a whole lot of excuses." I handed the chart back and added, "I recommend that you delete column G."

Dick deleted column G. And the results were nothing short of amazing.

Nineteen months later and seventy pounds lighter, Dick had shaved two hours and forty minutes off of his previous marathon time. He'd given up smoking and drinking. At fifty-two years old, he ran the Chicago Marathon in three hours and thirty-two minutes, a time that catapulted him to his dream: qualifying for the Boston Marathon.

Since then, Dick has run the Boston Marathon three times. He's become a role model for people who want to live healthier lives. His focus has shifted away from what he can't do and is now fixed on what he can do.

Dick deleted column G. Not just from his training spreadsheet. He deleted column G from his mental outlook.

He deleted negative excuses from his entire life.

Attitude: Envision Your Success

What is attitude? Why is it a key part of success?

Attitude is how you handle both your successes and your disappointments. You can think of it as your mental barometer. Attitude is the way you look at the world, the lens you use to experience life.

Attitude comes down to this choice: do you choose to look at the world in a positive light, or do you choose to look at it in a negative one? Those who view it in a positive light will be able to push through obstacles and hone the specific edge they're shooting for.

Attitude is one of the most underestimated keys of success out there. But a positive attitude can work wonders, just like it did with Dick. People with a positive mental outlook are much more successful than their negative counterparts.

A positive attitude gives you endurance in the business world. Disappointments are inevitable, and a lot of the time they're out of your control. But the attitude you have about those setbacks is not out of your control. Your attitude can be the deciding factor between giving up and giving it one more shot.

Taking control of your attitude is essential for achieving success. Even if a positive outlook doesn't come naturally to you, optimism is something that you can practice every day. Your attitude is the result of a conscious shift on your part. You develop it by finding the silver lining in setbacks, by surrounding yourself with positive people, by creating a supportive environment. Then you tap into it as a driving force on your way to success.

A positive attitude looks at obstacles and turns them into learning experiences. A positive attitude skips the excuses and goes straight to the solution. People with positive attitudes aren't content to be spectators in life. They want to be participants. They want to live lives filled with excitement and purpose.

Fifteen years ago, my wife Nannette and I went up to a natural hot springs in Colorado with our friends Carolyn and Larry Mugge. The only way to get to those springs was to cross-country ski the last two miles, so the spot attracted a very adventurous group.

The four of us skied up to the springs, and it was a truly magnificent setting. The steaming-hot water from the springs flowed into the icy-cold water of the river and created five natural hot-water pools in the riverbed. We picked a pool and relaxed for an hour. Then we got dressed and skied two miles back to the car before driving seven miles to Steamboat Springs for a beer at a local pub.

When we got to the pub, I realized that I was missing my wedding ring.

I never take off my ring on purpose, so I knew that it had slipped into the springs. Our group was about to be late for a dinner party. But I had priorities. I decided to go back for the ring. I'd hitchhike to the trailhead, ski back to the springs, search for my ring in the dark, and then return to meet the rest of the group for dinner as soon as I could.

All three of them thought I was crazy. But I had one thing going for me, and that was a positive attitude.

Sure enough, I found someone to give me a ride to the trailhead in about five minutes. I speed-skied back to the springs. Plenty of people were still up there, soaking in the pools. I told them what had happened and asked everyone to feel along the bottom of our pool in an effort to save my marriage.

Within three minutes, a voice yelled out in the darkness, "Found it!"

A spontaneous celebration broke out, and for the rest of the night everyone who heard the story could not believe how lucky I was. I didn't argue. But I didn't necessarily agree. I'd put myself in a position to be lucky by working hard and taking a risk.

I'd taken a positive attitude toward the situation. And it had paid off in the end.

To leverage the power of a positive attitude, you need to do three things: keep a positive focus, respond well to feedback, and be an "I can" person.

A Positive Focus

Are you focusing on the problem, or are you focusing on the solution?

A positive attitude is a critical tool for overcoming obstacles. It transforms disasters into opportunities to learn and grow, and it motivates you to come back better than ever before.

Consider where you fall on the following table:

Focus on problems	Focus on solutions
Search for excuses	Search for improvements
Stay stuck in the past	Look to the future
Think, "It was a failure"	Think, "It was a learning experience"
Find the negatives	Find the positives
Blame others	Accept responsibility
Be discouraged	Be motivated to improve
Act confidential	Act transparent
Cover up weaknesses	Address weaknesses

The road to success will probably be filled with disappointment. When those disappointments strike, your attitude is the thing that makes or breaks you. A positive attitude keeps you motivated, enthusiastic, and focused on the goal. It keeps you going, it keeps you improving, and it keeps you in line.

In the late 1990s, I worked with the Atlanta office of Deloitte on a business development plan. My idea was to target two major companies as ideal clients: Delta Airlines, because of our experience in the airline field; and the Southern Company, because of our experience with public utilities.

The senior partner responsible for the office thought I was crazy. "Both of those companies have been with their accounting firms for at least twenty-five years," he argued. "Those relationships are solid. They're untouchable."

"I understand that," I said, "but let's put Deloitte in their 'on deck' circles." I was optimistic. I pointed out that anything could happen. One of those companies might want a second opinion on something. A conflict of interest might come up. The partner at the competitive firm might retire, and they might not like the new partner. Or, with our international experience in both industries, we might be able to uncover an overlooked opportunity. As long as we placed ourselves in each company's on-deck circle, we'd be in a better position to win some business.

We gave the plan a shot. Two years later, we'd picked up a couple of small projects from both firms, but nothing significant.

Then the unthinkable happened. Arthur Anderson, the auditor for both companies, mishandled the relationship with Enron and was forced out of business. Deloitte was on deck when it happened, and that put us in the best position to pick up the business.

Because of our positive attitude, both Delta and Southern Company became audit clients for Deloitte.

The corporate world is full of situations like this one. Those who face them have the same choice we did. Are you going to let disappointment stop you in your tracks? Or are you going to use a positive attitude to conquer obstacles and keep moving forward?

Responding to Feedback

Attitude plays a major role in the way you respond to feedback. When you react to feedback in a positive way, you encourage growth and improvement. When you react negatively, the opposite is true.

People respond to constructive criticism in three different ways. The first is that they listen intently, internalize the problem, decide that they're a failure and a loser, and wonder how they're ever going to keep moving forward. These people usually recover after a good night's sleep by forgetting the criticism altogether.

The second common response to constructive feedback is to view the criticism as a personal attack that needs to be defended. "It wasn't my fault that it happened," these people say. "I was just doing what I was told to do. I can't help it if things went wrong." If the excuses don't work, they attack the messenger as an unfair individual who is hypercritical about everything. Their attitude is, "Someone has to be wrong, and it just can't be me."

The third and only productive response to constructive criticism is to listen, understand, confirm what you have heard, and immediately start exploring ways to correct the situation. This is the attitude that will help you improve yourself and your organization.

An easy way to make sure you have the right attitude for accepting constructive criticism when someone gives you feedback, before you even try to respond, is to ask yourself this question: "How could the comment be correct?" All too often, our automatic response to criticism is to defend ourselves by proving that the comment is wrong. But when we make a real effort to see the truth in critical feedback, we empower ourselves to reach new levels of improvement.

When you respond to constructive feedback with a positive attitude, you encourage people to keep giving you feedback. The more feedback you get, the stronger you become. That's the kind of outlook that generates advancement.

"I Can" versus "I Can't" People

My grandmother had a saying about negative people. She said, "Some people can find a bird dropping in any beautiful forest."

You attract positive people by having a positive attitude yourself, and the fastest way to develop your own positive attitude further is to surround yourself with positive people. By the same token, you have to stay clear of negative people, because they will bring you down. When you increase the time you spend with positive people and decrease the time you spend with negative people, you expedite your journey to success.

So who are the positives, and who are the negatives?

Some individuals have a natural tendency to focus on the negative instead of the positive. I refer to these individuals as "I can't" people. They go on vacation and harp on the one day that the weather was bad instead of all the days that the weather was really remarkable.

Then you have people on the other end of the spectrum, the "I can" people. These people focus on the positive. They don't have time for excuses. They direct their energy toward figuring out why they can do something instead of why they can't do it.

When I was head of marketing and sales for Omni Hotels Worldwide, I noticed that having positive people work with the guests could mean the difference between success and failure for the business. Positive people welcomed the guests' problems because they saw themselves as the solutions to those issues. They knew that they were being given the opportunity to make this person's day.

Negative employees saw guest complaints as annoying distractions that kept them from completing their work. I advised against hiring negative people for customer interaction roles because it made such a huge difference.

People with positive attitudes are more enthusiastic, more motivated, and more likely to find solutions to obstacles. When negative events occur, they use them as opportunities to improve the system. They keep the vision strong, and they keep the ball moving forward.

When you surround yourself with positive people, you invite success into your world.

Creating a Positive Environment

If you are the leader of an organization, create an environment that promotes a positive attitude among your people. This is one of the best things you can do to ensure success. A positive attitude is infectious. When you understand the power of positive thinking, you and your team can produce extraordinary results.

A big concept in the hospitality industry is known as the "mirror image." The idea behind the mirror image is simple: the way you treat your employees is the way those employees are going to treat your customers. If you have a positive attitude and treat your employees with respect, they're going to have a positive attitude and treat your customers with respect. If you chew your employee out in a disrespectful way and then send that person off to deal with customers, you can imagine what kind of service that customer is about to receive.

A positive environment is a productive environment. It's an atmosphere where people are happy in their roles. It inspires people to find solutions to problems instead of excuses to slow down progress.

Positive environments also attract and retain remarkable new talent. They are places where people want to work and train because they are recognized for doing things right. When everyone is motivated by the same positive outlook, success is the inevitable result.

The Power of Positive

Never underestimate the power of a positive outlook to guide you to success. A positive attitude changes the way you see the world. It pushes you to make the most of the opportunities that come your way, negative or positive. It motivates you to find solutions instead of excuses.

When you bring the right people with the right attitude together, you set yourself up for success. More than that, you set yourself up to enjoy the journey. The next chapter reveals another key tool you need to achieve your specific edge: enjoyment.

▲

CHAPTER SEVEN
Enjoy The Edge

You achieve success in your field when you don't know whether what you are doing is work or play.

WARREN BEATTY

Ironman: The Real Win

For the Ironman World Championship, I trained an average of twenty-five hours a week for eleven months. That fell in the range of forty miles of running, ten miles of swimming, and about two hundred miles of bike riding every seven days. That's enough exercise to make me a certifiable "fruitcake."

A big part of what kept me showing up for it every day were the seven or eight "fruitcake" groups that I trained with.

I had a group of swimmers. I had two groups of runners. I had three groups of bike riders. I even had a group of triathletes who did multiple things with me on the same day. All of them took my tough challenges and turned them into laughter and encouragement on a daily basis.

Wednesday was one of my favorite days. On Wednesdays, I drove up to the Budweiser brewery plant forty miles north of Atlanta with my triathlete group—the TriGeeks. We parked there, and then we took off. The first hour, we ran five to seven miles. The next two hours, we rode our bikes through thirty miles of beautiful farm country. Then we spent the last half hour swimming in Lake Altoona. Finally, we'd wrap up with a picnic to celebrate the exercise we'd done. I'd show up at my office at two in the afternoon and work until ten. And it was a great day.

Every step of my training was a great experience and a remarkable adventure.

I clearly remember the day I crossed the finish line and became second in the world in the Ironman World Championship. For a guy who had always been stuck in right field—if I got to play at all—that was a really big step for me. My wife was there at the finish line, and she put the winner's lei around my neck. We hugged, we walked, we celebrated. It was wonderful.

But the most satisfying moment for me wasn't the podium at the awards ceremony. It was turning on my computer three hours later to find over 150 emails waiting for me from my supporters—the people in my running groups, the people in my biking and swimming groups, the TriGeeks from the Wednesday triathlon group, and countless others. All of these people had stayed up past midnight Atlanta time to watch me finish my race and to share in my victory.

These were the people who had helped me celebrate what really mattered: the enjoyment of the journey, each step of the way. That journey changed my life. And I had loved every step of it.

What Is Enjoyment?

There are no shortcuts to success. Success requires a lot of discipline and hard work. That's why it's so important to love the work you're doing while you're doing it.

That's why it's so important to enjoy the journey.

Enjoyment is about the journey—the sustained effort that leads you to your specific edge. Often, the real satisfaction is the process of achieving a goal, not the end result itself. Enjoyment gives you the endurance to get where you're going. But more important than that, it reminds you to appreciate the passion that you're putting into getting there.

Too many people are in their jobs for the wrong reasons. They just show up for the paycheck. I call that a short-term solution. People who function that way will never excel. They just don't have the passion to be really good at what they're doing. They haven't learned that it's not about a job; it's about a career.

They haven't learned to enjoy the life they're building as they're building it.

Enjoyment is about celebrating your success. Not just the success of your ultimate goal, but of the milestones you reach along the way. Celebrating helps you preserve the positive mental attitude that you need to keep moving forward.

Enjoyment also benefits the people who are helping you work toward your goals. When you celebrate your successes, those people celebrate, too. They are recognized for their contributions, and they feel how important they are. Your team stays motivated, and your success keeps on rolling in.

At an Ironman event, most triathletes aren't interested in winning awards. They're interested in improving their performances and participating in an event that represents their personal accomplishments. After the competition, there's always a celebration just to honor everyone who completed the event.

Finishing an Ironman is winning. It's something that those athletes cherish for the rest of their lives. They buy T-shirts, hats, jackets, and license plate holders that celebrate the fact that they are Ironman finishers. Some even get Ironman logos tattooed on their legs as a permanent reminder of their accomplishment. That's enjoyment.

The concept of enjoyment is appearing more and more in the business world, as well. The new generation of the workforce grew up in an environment of celebration. They were on soccer teams as kids where they got trophies just for participating. They were recognized and rewarded for their efforts.

They were raised with an attitude of enjoyment, and that is changing the way business works. Companies are thinking of positive ways to keep the new generation of top performers motivated at work. Enjoyment isn't the exception anymore. It's becoming the rule.

Enjoyment Is a Journey, Not a Destination

When I was at Deloitte, one of the senior partners there was a running buddy of mine. This man was one of the most frugal individuals I knew. He and his wife had a goal, and that was for him to retire at sixty-two so that they could travel the world. She even worked as a travel agent to become more knowledgeable of all the great places they were going to travel to. They spent years building up a significant savings so that they could spend their retirement years going anywhere they wanted and enjoying themselves.

One week, this man went up to Philadelphia for a business meeting. The meeting ended at five o'clock in the afternoon, and dinner was scheduled for seven o'clock that evening. So he decided to go out for a run.

He went out for that run, and he came back from it. But he didn't show up to dinner at seven. At half past seven, they broke down the door to his hotel room. He'd had a fatal heart attack. He was gone.

Here was a guy who focused so much on the destination—of saving up for retirement—that I'm not sure he remembered to enjoy his time while he had it. He spent his life preparing for an event that he never lived to see.

Too many people are like my running buddy. They're chasing an ultimate dream, and in the meantime they don't enjoy the life they're living. They forget that you only get to do this once. You only get one chance to write your life story. You can't put the things you love on hold. You have to make them a priority. That's something you have to manage yourself, because no one else is going to manage it for you.

You have to enjoy where you're going while you're going there. You need to have a goal that is yours, a dream that is yours. And it has to be something that brings you a great sense of fulfillment as you are traveling toward your destination. That's how enjoyment carries you down the path to success.

To truly experience enjoyment on your journey, you need to move at the right pace, hang out with the right people, and be in the right place. You also need to strike a balance between enjoyment and work.

Try this exercise for fun. If you could live anywhere in the world when you retire, where would you live and why?

Now ask yourself this question: Why aren't you spending more time there now? Better yet, why aren't you already living there, or making plans to live there in the near future?

When you can identify the things holding you back, you can act to get rid of them—and you can clear a path to your own enjoyment.

The Three Ps of Enjoyment

People often come up to me after a speech and say, "Boy, I wish I could start a running program like yours," or "I wish I could build a bridge between an exercise program and my business." Plenty of them have tried in the past, but they couldn't keep it up because they didn't enjoy themselves.

I always encourage these people to focus on the three Ps of enjoyment: pace, people, and place.

Pace

Pace is the first P of enjoyment. With running, this is easy. Generally, if people can't stick to a running program, it's because it hurts too much. They're pushing too hard or too fast. They're in pain, and the benefit just isn't worth the discomfort. So I set this standard: if you can't talk to someone next to you while you're running, you're running too fast. And if you can sing while you're running, you're running too slow.

Business is the same way. I've seen eager beavers dive into a new assignment full-throttle, completely driven by their sense of urgency. A week or two later, they've burned themselves out.

In the first week of a new assignment, it's easy to be intimidated by the enormity of what needs to be done. So you have to set a steady pace from the start. Take the big task and chop it into smaller pieces. This saves you from being overwhelmed by the size of it.

People

The second P of enjoyment is people. Never underestimate the importance of camaraderie when it comes to enjoying the journey. This is absolutely true of running. Whenever I have an early morning run, I always make sure I'm supposed to meet someone else. That gives me an extra incentive to get out of bed, because I don't want somebody waiting for me in a parking lot at 5:30 a.m., only to have me not show up. Having a buddy to share with keeps you motivated in the long term.

People are just as important in business. Work becomes enjoyable when you surround yourself with team members who are positive, supportive, have dreams similar to yours, and are trying to make a difference.

Make people a priority in your company culture when you're looking for new opportunities. Build an environment that attracts people who are living exciting, multidimensional lives. When you work with people who you enjoy being around, you become more motivated, productive, and successful. The more successful you are, the more opportunities you'll get. Enjoyment becomes a process that fuels itself indefinitely.

Place

The third P of enjoyment is place. This one is really important to me. As a runner, where I run makes a difference. If I'm running along a river or through some woods, or even through a neighborhood of beautiful houses, the whole journey becomes that much more enjoyable. When I travel, I use my running regimen to explore new cities: New York, San Francisco, Portland, Chicago, Philadelphia. Even if you're on a treadmill, you still have the power to create an enjoyable environment just by turning on a television set or playing some good music. The environment brings enjoyment to the run.

Place is just as important in business—especially when it comes to the next generation. Gen Xers and Gen Yers put a lot of importance on where they live and work. They want a pleasant working environment, and that includes the atmosphere generated by the company culture. They want a place where they feel that they can make a difference. An enjoyable environment plays a huge role in that goal.

Stick to the three Ps for just about anything life throws at you. Choose the right pace, associate with supportive people, and create an environment that motivates you. Where the three Ps go, enjoyment follows.

The Balance Between Work and Enjoyment

There are always going to be things that you like to do and things that you have to do. Not everything will be fun and games. But everything should be about striking a balance between work and enjoyment.

I traveled a lot throughout my corporate career, especially when I was with Frito-Lay, Pepsi, and Deloitte. But in spite of my schedule, I made sure that every time I went to a new city, I reserved some time to explore.

Once when I visited Philadelphia for a conference, I grabbed a couple of the other attendees and said, "Let's take a run around the city in the morning." At six o'clock the next morning, we all went for a run. We were back at the hotel by seven and ready for the conference at eight o'clock sharp. But in the meantime, we saw Independence Hall. We saw the Liberty Bell. We watched the sun come up as we crossed the Benjamin Franklin Bridge. We were there for a business conference, but we made room for enjoyment anyway.

Vacation time is another area where work and enjoyment find balance. I touched on this in chapter 6. Too many people come up with all kinds of excuses not to take their vacation time. They're looking for recognition, or they think they're indispensable. But I have never seen anyone recognized for forgoing their vacation, and I have never seen anyone fired for taking it. Use your vacation to enjoy yourself. Then come back to work with a fully charged battery.

Leading Enjoyment

The responsibility for creating an enjoyable work environment falls in part on the individual. But the other part of that responsibility falls on the leaders running the organizations.

Leaders have an obligation to create an environment where people want to work. Research indicates that people who work in enjoyable environments are more motivated and more productive than people who don't. Companies that create an environment of enjoyment are the ones that attract the best and the brightest.

Enjoyment on the Edge

People who enjoy what they do are more successful at what they're doing. They wake up every morning feeling enthusiastic about the challenges they're going to face. They're motivated to excel in their fields. They share their successes and they celebrate their triumphs. They're passionate about their long-term goals.

They live meaningful lives filled with excitement and purpose, and they inspire everyone around them to do the same.

When you incorporate enjoyment into your process, you've pushed your evolution as a cutting-edge entrepreneur to amazing heights. There's just one more benchmark on the path to your specific edge. That benchmark is being able to anticipate.

*Anticipation is leveraging
what you know to
predict the future.*

MIKE WIEN

▲

CHAPTER EIGHT
Anticipate Success

---

*Future success is found in anticipating
the needs of your <u>ideal</u> customer.*

DICK WOODEN

Raising the Bar

The journey to my first Ironman World Championship was a three-year process. It started with training for my first-ever Ironman in Florida, continued as I trained for the world-championship qualifier in Wisconsin, and ended at the Ironman World Championship itself in Kona, Hawaii.

Over those three years, I put a lot of focus on becoming a better swimmer, cyclist, and runner. I developed the discipline to improve. With all that training, I certainly built up my endurance. I also made sure I kept the rest of my life balanced, I maintained a positive attitude, and I definitely enjoyed the ride. All the while, I kept pushing toward my ultimate goal: to finish in the top five on the podium at the end of the day.

Finally, after three years, three Ironmans, and countless other races, I did it. I stood in fifth place on the podium as a top Ironman competitor in my age group at the world championship.

The thrill was unbelievable. All the 5:00 a.m. runs in the rain, the grueling bike rides in ninety-plus-degree heat, the hours, the failures, the triumphs, the years—everything I'd been through had finally paid off.

I had reached my goal.

Not long after the race ended and I had finally pulled it together emotionally, I wandered over to the pizza tent to catch up on lost calories. Before I had taken a single bite, Fox Ferrel—the leader of the TriGeeks from Atlanta and another Kona finisher—came up to me. He gave me a big hug. Then he asked, "So Mike, what's next?"

I looked at Fox, and that was when it hit me. I didn't know.

I had spent the previous three years focused on my ultimate dream, raising the bar after every successful milestone. But now, raising the bar to a higher goal seemed out of the question.

Then Dick Jones—the same guy who created "Column G" in his exercise tracking sheet—called me up. He wanted to qualify for the Boston Marathon, and he asked if I would give him feedback. I was happy to help.

Months later, when Dick reached his goal and qualified for the marathon in Boston, I was almost as excited about his accomplishment as I'd been about my own title in the Ironman World Championship. And that was when I realized what I had become for Dick. A mentor. I understood that I could help other people live out their dreams.

I had a new goal. Helping others create lives full of meaning and purpose became the key to achieving meaning and purpose myself. To help others, I realized I had to get back in the game. I resumed training for Ironman with a new personal goal in mind.

The anticipation I felt for others rebooted my energy, my passion, and my purpose in life.

Mission Accomplished—Now What?

You've been through all the steps on the path to success. You've set your goal. You've concentrated your focus on a specialization. You've practiced discipline. You've endured. You've kept that endurance going with balance and enjoyment, and you've accomplished what you set out to do.

You've earned the success you dreamed of in the beginning. This is when the question arises: Now what?

Now you can convert your knowledge and experience into a powerful tool: anticipating the future.

Anticipating has to do with the "edge" part of your specific edge. To have an edge, you have to outsmart, outplay, and outmaneuver your competition. When you anticipate, you understand the competition's strengths and weaknesses. You also understand your own strengths and weaknesses. And you understand your customers' needs so well that you can serve them before they ever ask to be served.

That's the kind of competitive edge that gets you the success you're looking for.

One of the greatest hockey players of all time is Wayne Gretzky. Wayne was asked in an interview what his secret to success was. He replied, "I skate to where the puck is going to be, not to where it has been." That's anticipation.

Anticipation is the ultimate level of success. You reach this level when you become so knowledgeable in your specialization that you see the way forward before anyone else does. Your horizon stretches farther than that of your competitors, and you become a resource to others.

Mentoring is a form of anticipation. In business, it grows rising stars by leveraging the talents of old pros. When you pass the torch this way, you help others anticipate the future. You can also mentor your customers by anticipating their needs and showing them the best path of action.

Anticipation is leveraging what you know to predict the future. Being able to anticipate gives you one of the strongest competitive advantages you can have in business. You know your customers so well, you can give them what they want before they even know they want it. You can provide answers to questions that they didn't think of asking. You can identify solutions to problems they didn't know they had. And you can uncover opportunities for them that they overlooked.

I think of anticipation as the fifth level of marketing. To leverage it, you need to understand the first four levels, as well.

The Five Levels of Marketing

I spent twenty-eight years working in corporate America, and in that time I realized that pretty much any business could be broken down into certain levels of marketing. I call these the five levels of marketing. The higher the level of your organization, the more you'll be able to differentiate yourself from your competitors, and the more success you'll see.

Let me take you through each of the five levels.

Level 1: Produce. Say you're a farmer who grows corn. You grow your corn, and your field happens to be near a road, so you set up a stand to sell the corn. When people drive by and see the stand, they stop and buy corn from you. This is the first level of marketing: production.

Level 2: Promote. In the second level of marketing, you realize that you could get more people to stop and buy your corn if they knew what a great deal it was. So you put up a sign in front of your stand that says "Corn: 4 ears for $1." You're promoting your corn to the market. Sure enough, more people stop to buy corn. Promotion takes many forms, including billboards, advertising, social media, and public relations. Around 5 percent of businesses are at levels 1 and 2.

Level 3: Sell. Now you decide that you're ready to sell your corn to more than just the people who happen to drive down the road. So you put your son on his bicycle with a couple dozen ears of corn in the basket and you send him into town with it. He rides up and down the street selling corn. Now you're selling your product—the third level of marketing. Companies with large sales forces that have sales quotas are excellent examples of level 3 organizations. About 40 percent of businesses are at this level.

Level 4: Respond. By this point, you have a lot of people buying corn, and you want to make your business stronger. You'll sell more corn if you give the people the kind of corn they want. So you ask them, "Why do you buy your corn from a corn stand instead of a supermarket?" And you find out that they like the fact that it is country fresh. They also tell you that they would love to buy things besides produce from the country, like baked goods and jams. Just like that, you have the opportunity to expand your offerings to meet their demands and increase your sales. The fourth level of marketing is respond, and another 40 percent of companies are at this level. They survey their customers. They're responsive to customer requests. They're sensitive about customer service, and they understand the trends.

Level 5: Anticipate. Finally, after you've been through the other four levels of marketing, you reach the fifth level: anticipate. This is where all organizations need to be. These are the companies that attract the best and the brightest talent. Only 15 percent of companies have reached the fifth level of marketing.

But before you can really understand the fifth level of marketing, you need to understand how the consumer's mind works. The best way to do that is to have a clear grasp of the four quadrants of knowledge.

The Four Quadrants of Knowledge

You Know What You Know	**You Know What You Don't Know**
You Don't Know What You Know	**You Don't Know What You Don't Know**

Take a look at the chart above. The first of the four quadrants of knowledge is simple: you know what you know. Let's use the example of computers. You know you have a computer, and you know how to use it. Really straightforward—you know what you know.

Then you have the second quadrant of knowledge: you know what you don't know. Now your computer breaks, and you don't know how to fix it. You know that you don't have the knowledge to take care of this on your own, and you need to call someone in to fix it. That's not a problem, because you know what you don't know.

The third quadrant of knowledge gets interesting: you don't know what you know. This quadrant represents your instincts. Maybe you've never had any official training, but you can figure out how to get something done anyway. If the fire alarm goes off, you may not have studied the emergency escape plan in advance, but you're still going to find a way out of the building. Or you install an unfamiliar program on your computer, but you're familiar with enough other programs that you know where the start button is, and you can get it up and running.

Finally, you have the fourth quadrant of knowledge: you don't know what you don't know. This is your danger zone. This is where you can get blindsided. This is where organizations should be focused: on what their clients don't know that they don't know.

Now we can take it back to the fifth level of marketing, because the fifth level of marketing revolves around this same concept: you don't know what you don't know. No one realizes that there's a problem, an inconvenience, or a missed opportunity. You show them a better way. You give them what they didn't even know they needed.

You anticipate their needs before they can tell you that they need something.

When you anticipate, you reach a much higher level as an organization. Anticipation differentiates you from your competition. That makes you more effective and drives you toward success.

One of the best examples of a company anticipating the needs of its clients in recent years is Apple. In 2006, how many people called their cell phone company and said, "You know, I really hate these buttons. Can you develop a touch screen?" No one. Apple saw the value of that product before the consumer realized that it was a possibility. The company anticipated its clients' needs before their clients did. It released the iPhone in 2007 and saw enormous success.

Another excellent example of this is the cable manufacturing giant Southwire. In 2011, the southeast experienced an upswing of copper thievery. As the value of copper increased, Southwire's clients discovered that high volumes of copper cables were being stolen and resold to recycling agencies. The theft threatened public safety and the power supply.

Southwire used the copper-theft epidemic to anticipate its customers' needs and find a solution. The company created a new product called "Proof Positive® Copper with Trace ID Technology." The new copper was etched with unique laser IDs that linked back to a database. When recyclers purchased copper, they were able to scan the ID to see if it had been stolen. If it was, they could identify the person who'd delivered the stolen copper to the authorities.

Within a few weeks of the product's release, three copper thieves were arrested, and stealing copper was on its way to becoming a problem of the past. By caring about its customers' troubles, understanding the industry, and committing resources to coming up with a solution, Southwire gained a competitive advantage over its competitors and solidified its relationship with its clients.

Learn to Anticipate

So how do you learn to anticipate? What are the techniques and strategies you can use to reach that all-important fifth level of marketing? How do you provide answers to your clients' questions before they think of asking them?

You leverage the power of everything you built to get you to your goal.

The journey toward success has made you into a remarkable specialist. You are dealing with a very specific type of customer, and there are thousands or maybe even millions of customers with the same problem. Your detailed knowledge of your field gives you insight into advancements that your client base doesn't have access to yet.

In other words, you notice that people are having trouble punching the buttons on their phones. You are also aware of touchscreen technology. You put those two things together into a solution that nobody else saw coming. That's the power of anticipating solutions.

The most successful companies and individuals know how to anticipate. Say you are a software company that provides online customer services to community banks. Your specific focus creates a competitive advantage for your business. You've been working with community banks all over the country since online banking became popular, and your service eliminates the state-of-the-art technological advantage that larger banks once had over community banks.

Since you work with so many community banks, you see which sites work for them and which don't. You also track what the big banks are doing, and that puts you in a great position to anticipate your clients' needs. You develop new software and services to keep them up to speed with their big-bank competition. You help them become more successful. You build a high level of trust with them. Then when you go to sell your new software, your anticipation wins you more than that one sale. It wins you a great client for life.

One example of a company that has really turned anticipation into a fine art is Target. Target has a very sophisticated frequent-shoppers program. The company can predict all kinds of things based on its customers' shopping habits. One of the things it can predict is when a woman gets pregnant. It can do that based on a number of items she buys, such as hand towels, sanitizers, and unscented products. Not only can Target predict that someone is pregnant, it can also pretty much predict what that person's due date is.

Target can then send coupons to new mothers that are ideal for what they're going to need. The company knows exactly what to send when the child turns six months old, one year old, and so on.

Target's model is so good that the organization even got into a little bit of trouble with it, because it was able to predict that someone was pregnant before that person had broken the news to anybody else in the family. Now, Target includes those maternity coupons inside of a general coupon book so that it's not as obvious that the person receiving them is being targeted as a new mother.

Another great example of a company that knows how to anticipate the needs of its clients is Home Depot. Whenever a natural disaster appears on the horizon, Home Depot sets up a war room in its headquarters before the disaster strikes. In the war room, its organizers anticipate the products and staff that will be needed. Then they make plans to relocate both the products and the people to the disaster area as soon as possible.

I once met a Home Depot executive, and I talked to him about this. I commented that devastations like snowstorms and hurricanes were terrible, but at the same time, the company must generate a lot of business.

The executive said, "We do sell a lot of products. But, you know, the expense of getting that store open, bringing in all of the employees, and transporting stock in from all over the country . . . honestly, the cost there more than offsets any additional profit we bring in. We actually lose money. But here's why we do it. Our customers need those materials. They walk over to one of our competitors and those guys are sold out. They don't have the snow shovel; they don't have the generator. Then the same customers come to our store, and we have what they desperately need. That earns us a loyal customer for life."

Home Depot knows that anticipation earns you an ongoing relationship with your customers. You can shoot for the low-hanging fruit and pick it once. Or you can make an investment, anticipate the needs of your clients, and harvest the whole tree.

Anticipation Is Your Specific Edge

When you can anticipate someone else's needs, you have reached the pinnacle of your profession. You have achieved the highest level of marketing, and you have found a competitive advantage.

You have earned a powerful specific edge.

Learning to anticipate is not a short-term strategy. It takes time and effort to gain the knowledge and experience that will allow you to offer this insight. But when you do, the results are staggering. Anticipation positions you as a valuable resource or a trusted advisor. And that makes anticipation the final key to your specific edge.

Always be passionate and purposeful about life. Always make a difference. Always believe that the best is still to come.

MIKE WIEN

▲

CHAPTER NINE
The Finish Line

We make a living by what we get;
we make a life by what we give.

WINSTON CHURCHILL

The Cheers Before Seventeen Hours

One of the greatest things about an Ironman is the final hour of the race.

The race officially begins at 7:00 a.m. and ends at 12:00 a.m. the next day, exactly seventeen hours after it starts. If you cross the finish line at seventeen hours and two seconds, it doesn't count. You have to get there before the clock hits midnight to finish the race.

The organizers set up bleachers at the finish line. Those bleachers aren't for people to welcome in the pros who cross the line in eight hours. The pros don't attract the big crowd. The big crowd at an Ironman really shows up around eleven o'clock at night. Why?

Because people want to be there to cheer on the competitors who won't quit.

They want to cheer on the people who have been fighting for hours to live the dream of becoming an Ironman; the people who are trying to prove that they have the ultimate endurance to overcome anything. They want to cheer on the people who have been out there for sixteen-and-a-half hours and are still pushing all the way to the end. These are the people who know that finishing is winning. At an Ironman, the real thrill isn't being there for the first-place finish.

At an Ironman, the real thrill is being there at a quarter to midnight, when the crowd comes out to bring home the real champions, and the final cheers before that seventeen-hour mark go up.

No Shortcuts

Now that you have the formula for success, it's time to put it into practice. Like my Tri-Geek buddy Fox Ferrel likes to say, "Are we gonna talk, or are we gonna ride?" It's time to start riding.

Find your passion and set your goal based on what you love to do. Hone that passion into a specific edge to give you a competitive advantage in the market. Practice discipline to gain the knowledge and techniques that will put you at the top of your game. Endure in the face of hard obstacles, and keep moving forward.

Through it all, maintain balance in your life. Enjoy the journey, and bring the people you care about along for the ride. Hold on to a positive attitude on the dark days, and become so skilled at what you do that you can anticipate what comes next. Then give back by sharing your knowledge with others.

Shoot for the finish line, and achieve success.

Come Out of the Box

With all this knowledge and a solid understanding of the route to success, where do you start? Here are ten steps to get you on the road, not just to success in the business world, but also to an exciting, passionate, and purposeful life.

1. Make a short list of the things you most enjoy doing. Pursue what you are good at, what you are passionate about, and what you can see yourself doing in the future.

2. Establish a goal that focuses on what you identified in the first step. Then share that dream with others so that they can support you, encourage you, and give you advice. Their support will boost your commitment to your goal.

3. Develop a plan with plenty of intermediate steps or milestones to lead you in the right direction.

4. Create a way to track your performance.

5. Start the journey with small steps.

6. Bring others with you. Find people who have similar goals. Encourage them. Train with them. Share stories and best practices. Maybe even mentor them. If they are part of your team or organization at work, help them to feel ownership in the goal.

7. Celebrate your successes at each milestone as you work toward your goal.

8. Be willing to adjust and fine-tune your goals and methods.

9. Make it a priority to have fun and keep your life in balance.

10. Find time to help others live their dreams along the way.

Your Olympic Potential

Every two years, the world's best athletes gather to compete in the Olympic Games. We cheer on these men and women and draw inspiration from the incredible paths they traveled for a chance to stand on the Olympic podium.

When we listen to their stories, we see a common thread emerge. Every Olympic athlete specializes in a very explicit sport. These individuals are focused and have given up a lot to chase their dreams. They're disciplined in their rigorous training schedules, and they surround themselves with coaches who suggest ideas to improve. They track their performances and look for ways to make them better. Many rely on large support groups of family and friends to keep them on track and to keep things in perspective. And they have all overcome adversity and pushed past disappointments.

Olympic athletes show us all the critical attributes of being successful in whatever you choose to do. They show us that with these attributes, anything is possible.

When you embody these qualities, you become the star Olympian in your own life. In sports, business, or anything else, you have the power to be your own champion. You have what it takes to achieve your specific edge.

The Kona Coffee Company

Ironman triathletes are people who believe in participating in life to the fullest. Every year during the Ironman World Championship in Hawaii, the Kona Coffee Company sets up a free coffee bar open Monday through Friday, from seven to nine o'clock in the morning. That coffee bar is a gathering place for a lot of triathletes to visit for a little bit over a cup of coffee, then leave and go about their days. But there's one thing about that Kona Coffee bar that makes it unique, and that's the location.

The Kona Coffee bar is located half a mile out in the middle of Kona Bay, and swimming is the only way to get there.

Most of the triathletes at the Ironman World Championship choose to make that swim. And when they get to the boat, they don't climb up on deck and take a breather. Someone hands the coffee cup down to them over the side and they tread water while they drink it.

Now I ask you, where else in the world could they set up a free coffee bar half a mile out in the middle of the ocean, and everybody thinks that it's a great idea? Only in Hawaii during Ironman week, because these people have a zest for what they do. These people believe in living every experience to the fullest.

These people know the power of creating an exciting and purposeful life.

The Best Is Still to Come

As of this writing, I am sixty-two years old. I believe today that my best Ironman is still ahead of me.

I know too many fifty-year-olds who are just trying to hang on to where they were when they were forty. That's the kind of thinking that holds you back from achieving the lifelong dreams you deserve.

Never tell yourself that your best days are behind you. Tell yourself that your best days still lie ahead, because that's the truth. Keep improving. Keep pushing toward new achievements and new heights. Look for a way to write a new life chapter that is even more meaningful than the last.

Always be on a journey with a goal ahead of you. Always be passionate and purposeful about life. Always make a difference.

Always believe that the best is still to come.

Turtles on the Road

When I trained for Ironman, I rode my bike anywhere from 150 to 250 miles a week. Most of those bike rides were out in the woods or through farm country. And occasionally, as I rode along, I came across a turtle sitting in the middle of the road.

When a turtle starts across the road in the middle of a hot day, one of two things usually happens. One, the turtle overheats and fries on the hot asphalt. Or two, it gets hit by a car.

So whenever I saw a turtle on the road during my bike rides, I stopped. I picked it up, and I moved it off the asphalt to safety. Maybe it was grateful for the help. Maybe not. But I felt good about myself for the rest of the day. I had made a difference. I had helped someone out of harm's way.

Each of us comes upon our share of turtles in the road as we go through life. Maybe yours is the person training for that all-important race who needs the encouragement to go the extra mile. Maybe it's the colleague at work who needs help finding the silver lining in a tough setback. Maybe it's the client who is looking for creative ways to reduce operating expenses and grow sales.

Whoever those people are for you, lend a helping hand. Lift them up. Help them figure out where the other side of the road is so that they can get there on their own.

When you help other people, good things happen. Your own skills improve as you teach them to others. You create a positive experience; one that often comes back around when the people you helped do something nice for you in return. You build trust with your clients, which opens the door for you to provide more products or services to fill their needs. And those loyal clients then recommend you to new people.

When you help others, you create a positive environment both for them and for yourself. You live life with more passion, greater meaning, and a stronger purpose. Most of all, you embrace the principles of success, and you encourage others to do the same.

You understand the power of your specific edge.

When you help other people,
good things happen.

MIKE WIEN

▲

About the Author
Mike Wien

Mike Wien is a professional speaker, consultant, and world-class athlete. He coaches entrepreneurs and business leaders to master the power of endurance, discipline, and a specific edge for success. As a former corporate leader, he held senior marketing and sales positions with Frito-Lay, PepsiCo, Omni Hotels, Citibank, and Deloitte. While at Frito-Lay, he was responsible for launching one of the most successful food brands: Tostitos®. In 2003, Wien founded The Specific Edge Institute, where he coaches high-performance leaders and their teams to achieve breakthrough results.

As an Ironman triathlete, Wien applies the skills of athletic competition to business success. He has competed in thirty-five marathons, including the Boston Marathon, the New York Marathon, the Chicago Marathon, and the original marathon from Marathon, Greece to Athens. He has also competed in nine Ironman triathlons, including four world championships in Kona, Hawaii. In 2011, he finished second in the world for his age group at the Ironman World Championship. His sponsors include Timex, PowerBar, Trek Bikes, and K-Swiss shoes.

Wien is also an adjunct professor of marketing in the Cecil B. Day School of Hospitality at Georgia State University and serves on four not-for-profit boards, including USA Triathlon under the US Olympic Committee, where he is vice president. He has an MBA in marketing from the Kellogg School at Northwestern University and a BS in business from Colorado State University. Wien lives in Atlanta, Georgia with his wife Nannette.

▲

Gain Your Specific Edge

Let Mike Wien show you how to gain *your* specific edge.

A professional speaker, consultant, and world-class athlete, Wien coaches entrepreneurs and business leaders to master the power of endurance, discipline, and a specific edge for success.

He delivers his powerful and inspiring message through keynote speeches, workshops and online communities.

Keynote Speeches

Wien's keynote speech "Sustained Effort Wins!" teaches audiences that:

- Direction beats speed
- Enjoyment makes your path as great as your goal
- If you reach all of your goals, they're not high enough
- Success is built on overcoming adversity
- You've got to keep moving forward

Call for Mike Wien's keynote speeches and talks.

Workshops

Through the Specific Edge Institute, Wien offers Specific Edge Workshops that help experienced professionals meet their goals. Participants learn how to:

- Harness the power of being specific
- Identify a strategic advantage
- Focus on the best targets
- Develop a compelling message
- Deliver that message for maximum impact

Call to learn more about Mike Wien's workshops and coaching programs.

Online Communities

Be inspired! Meet others who are using their specific edge and sustained effort to win. Nominate others you think deserve acknowledgments.

- **The Specific Edge Hall of Fame** – Showcasing people and companies that are leveraging a specific edge to their competitive advantage.

- **The Sustained Effort Hall of Fame** – Featuring individuals who have overcome significant obstacles to achieve success.

*Join these inspiring communities at **www.specificedge.com**.*

Contact:

www.mikewien.com
www.specificedge.com
(770) 518-0711
mike@specificedge.com
Facebook: www.facebook.com/mike.wien
Twitter: @Mike_Wien
LinkedIn: www.linkedin.com/in/mikewien